Robert Graves'
Poems
About Love

CASSELL · LONDON

CASSELL & COMPANY LTD
35 RED LION SQUARE, LONDON, WC1
Melbourne, Sydney, Toronto, Johannesburg, Auckland

S.B.N. 304 93494 1
Reprinted offset in Great Britain by
The Camelot Press Ltd., London and Southampton
F.769

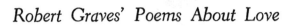

Robert Graves' Poems About Love

Foreword

These poems chosen from more than twenty books published in the past half-century are here printed in roughly chronological order, most of them being variations on the main poetic problem: which is how to restore the lost age of love-innocence between men and women.

Civilization seems to have begun as an enhancement not only of mother love, but of personal love-pacts; which in time brought about the ritual foundation of gift-exchanging clans and tribes. Ancient nations decayed as soon as a weakening of its individual love-pacts and love-treaties made the central religious authority harden into impersonal law; after which religion itself slowly faded. Yet even nowadays an archaic sense of love-innocence recurs, however briefly, among most young men and women. Some few of these, who become poets, remain in love for the rest of their lives, watching the world with a detachment unknown to lawyers, politicians, financiers, and all other ministers of that blind and irresponsible successor to matriarch and patriarchy—the mechanarchy.

Poets understand love as the union of complementary souls, an ecstatic event which sets the world on fire and allows them to transcend the loveless limits of time, space and circumstance. Love poems perpetuate this mystic moment. Poems about love, as a rule, either sadly or satirically record its defeat by practical circumstance.

Poetic faith may be proved logically untenable, but poets are not logicians. Although aware that man-woman love began as sexual courtship, they cannot regard its physical consummation as more than a metaphor for love itself, and refuse to let courtship degenerate into marital routine. And although the birth of children, though greeted at first with delight, may force lovers apart and involve them as parents in unnatural obedience to the mechanarchy, yet poets cannot disown their children. Nor can they renounce physical union as irrelevant to mystic union; still less, while reserving spiritual love for the beloved, can they take random bedfellows to ease a physical frustration.

Nevertheless, poets look forward to a final reign of love-innocence when the so-called impracticable will once more become the inevitable, when miracles are accepted without surprise or question, and when the patently illogical Machine has at last performed its *reductio ad absurdum*, by disintegrating.

Omar Khayyam in a quatrain omitted by FitzGerald from his 'adaptation' of the *Rubaiyat* writes:

> The Moon by her own nature prone to change
> Varies from animal form to vegetable.
> Destroy her form, you have destroyed nothing;
> For what she seems survives her not yet being.

The Moon here is Woman, with a temperament influenced by her menstrual period and by the Moon itself: she changes from the thin crescent moon which resembles a horn or tusk, to the full moon which suggests a melon or gourd; sometimes she shows fierce animal passion, sometimes she is easy-going and placid as a garden vegetable. She cannot in either condition be changed by male precept or persuasion. Khayyam's sharpest line is the last: he means that men believe in her love, and that this belief, although erroneous, remains active even when she has failed to love with the pure and faithful devotion offered her: because it secretly points to a time when women will not dissemble, lie or cheat in love. In Omar's day, the early twelfth century, Moslem women were, almost everywhere except in Berber countries, left uneducated, treated as chattels, and allowed no freedom in love. But Khayyam can do nothing about the general situation: he can only prophesy that she will one day BE in the true love sense.

Each of the love poems printed here commemorated a secret occasion and was written solely for whoever inspired it. Once these events had passed into history, the poems circulated and took on a life of their own, though still printed above my name; and I am embarrassed to take credit for work to which I can have only a partial, if nominal, claim. The numerous poems about lost love supply the thorny background, a warning of its intractability and, if it were not for the love-poems, might well read as evidence of ingratitude to life—against which, however, because I myself chose to be born, I have never lodged any ingrateful protest. Since poetry should not be confused with autobiography I refrain from marking

6

large groups with names of the women who inspired or provoked them. It would lead only to mischief.

My education has been Classical, and my family tradition Anglo-Irish; so here is an introductory poem addressed to the Celtic Hercules known to the Greek historian Lucian as Ogmian Hercules. The early Irish *ollamhs*, or master-poets, called him Ogma Sun-Face. He was their patron, under the Triple Muse-Goddess Brigit, inventor of their sacred Ogham alphabet, and represented as white-haired:

> Your Labours are performed, your Bye-works too,
> Your ashes gently drift from Oeta's peak.
> Here is escape then, Hercules, from empire.
>
> Lithe Hebë, youngest of all Goddesses,
> Who circles on the Moon's broad threshing-floor
> Harboured no jealousy for Megara,
> Augë, Hippolytë, Deianeira,
> But grieved for each in turn. You broke all hearts,
> Burning too Sun-like for a Grecian bride.
>
> Rest your immortal head on Hebë's lap;
> What wars you started let your sons conclude.
> Meditate a new Alphabet, heal wounds,
> Draw poets to you with long golden chains
> But still go armed with club and lion's pelt.

ROBERT GRAVES

Deyá, Mallorca, Spain, 1968

Contents

9

Part Two

Part Three

Part Four

Part Five

Part Six

Part Seven

Part Eight

Part Nine

Part 1

THE FINDING OF LOVE

Pale at first and cold,
Like wizard's lily-bloom
Conjured from the gloom,
Like torch of glow-worm seen
Through grasses shining green
By children half in fright,
Or Christmas candlelight
Flung on the outer snow,
Or tinsel stars that show
Their evening glory
With sheen of fairy story—

Now with his blaze
Love dries the cobweb maze
Dew-sagged upon the corn,
He brings the flowering thorn,
Mayfly and butterfly,
And pigeons in the sky,
Robin and thrush,
And the long bulrush,
Bird-cherry under the leaf,
Earth in a silken dress,
With end to grief,
With joy in steadfastness.

ONE HARD LOOK

Small gnats that fly
In hot July
And lodge in sleeping ears,
Can rouse therein
A trumpet's din
With Day of Judgement fears.

Small mice at night
Can wake more fright
Than lions at midday;
A straw will crack
The camel's back—
There is no easier way.

One smile relieves
A heart that grieves
Though deadly sad it be,
And one hard look
Can close the book
That lovers love to see.

SULLEN MOODS

Love, never count your labour lost
   Though I turn sullen or retired
Even at your side; my thought is crossed
   With fancies by no evil fired.

And when I answer you, some days
   Vaguely and wildly, never fear
That my love walks forbidden ways,
   Snapping the ties that hold it here.

If I speak gruffly, this mood is
   Mere indignation at my own
Shortcomings, plagues, uncertainties:
   I forget the gentler tone.

You, now that you have come to be
   My one beginning, prime and end,
I count at last as wholly me,
   Lover no longer nor yet friend.

Help me to see you as before
   When overwhelmed and dead, almost,
I stumbled on your secret door
   Which saves the live man from the ghost.

Be once again the distant light,
   Promise of glory, not yet known
In full perfection—wasted quite
   When on my imperfection thrown.

LOVE WITHOUT HOPE

Love without hope, as when the young bird-catcher
Swept off his tall hat to the Squire's own daughter,
So let the imprisoned larks escape and fly
Singing about her head, as she rode by.

THE TROLL'S NOSEGAY

A simple nosegay! was that much to ask?
(Winter still nagged, with scarce a bud yet showing.)
He loved her ill, if he resigned the task.
'Somewhere,' she cried, 'there must be blossom blowing.'
It seems my lady wept and the troll swore
By Heaven he hated tears: he'd cure her spleen—
Where she had begged one flower he'd shower fourscore,
A bunch fit to amaze a China Queen.

Cold fog-drawn Lily, pale mist-magic Rose
He conjured, and in a glassy cauldron set
With elvish unsubstantial Mignonette
And such vague bloom as wandering dreams enclose.
But she?
   Awed,
     Charmed to tears,
        Distracted,
           Yet—
Even yet, perhaps, a trifle piqued—who knows?

UNICORN AND THE WHITE DOE

Unicorn with burning heart
    Breath of love has drawn
On his desolate peaks apart
    At rumour of dawn,

Has trumpeted his pride
    These long years mute,
Tossed his horn from side to side,
    Lunged with his foot.

Like a storm of sand has run
    Breaking his own boundaries,
Gone in hiding from the sun
    Under camphor trees.

Straight was the course he took
    Across the plain, but here with briar
And mire the tangled alleys crook;
    Baulking desire.

A shoulder glinted white—
    The bough still shakes—
A white doe darted out of sight
    Through the forest brakes.

Tall and close the camphors grow,
    The grass grows thick—
Where you are I do not know,
    You fly so quick.

Where have you fled from me?
    I pursue, you fade,
I hunt, you hide from me
    In the tangled glade.

Often from my hot lair
    I would watch you drink
(A mirage of tremulous air,)
    From the pool's brink.

Vultures, always rocking high
  By the western gate,
Warned me with discordant cry
You were even such as I:
  You had no mate.

THE HILLS OF MAY

Walking with a virgin heart
  The green hills of May,
Me, the Wind, she took as lover
  By her side to play,

Let me toss her untied hair,
  Let me shake her gown,
Careless though the daisies redden,
  Though the Sun frown,

Scorning in her gay habit
  Lesser love than this,
My cool spiritual embracing,
  My secret kiss.

So she walked, the proud lady,
  So danced or ran,
So she loved with a whole heart,
  Neglecting man. . . .

Fade, fail, innocent stars
  On the green of May:
She has left our bournes for ever,
  Too fine to stay.

LOST LOVE

His eyes are quickened so with grief,
He can watch a grass or leaf
Every instant grow; he can
Clearly through a flint wall see,
Or watch the startled spirit flee
From the jaws of a dead man.
  Across two counties he can hear
And catch your words before you speak;
The woodlouse or the maggot's weak
Clamour rings in his sad ear,
And noise so slight it would surpass
Credence—drinking sound of grass,
Worm talk, clashing jaws of moth
Chumbling holes in cloth;
The groan of ants who undertake
Gigantic loads for honour's sake
(Their sinews creak, their breath comes thin),
Whir of spiders when they spin,
And minute whispering, mumbling, sighs
Of idle grubs and flies.
  This man is quickened so with grief,
He wanders god-like or like thief
Inside and out, below, above,
Without relief seeking lost love.

LOVE IN BARRENNESS

Below the ridge a raven flew
And we heard the lost curlew
Mourning out of sight below.
Mountain tops were touched with snow;
Even the long dividing plain
Showed no wealth of sheep or grain,
But fields of boulders lay like corn
And raven's croak was shepherd's horn
To slow cloud-shadow strayed across
A pasture of thin heath and moss.

The North Wind rose: I saw him press
With lusty force against your dress,
Moulding your body's inward grace
And streaming off from your set face;
So now no longer flesh and blood
But poised in marble flight you stood.
O wingless Victory, loved of men,
Who could withstand your beauty then?

SONG OF CONTRARIETY

Far away is close at hand,
Close joined is far away,
Love shall come at your command
Yet will not stay.

At summons of your dream-despair
She might not disobey,
But slid close down beside you there,
And complaisant lay.

Yet now her flesh and blood consent
In the hours of day,
Joy and passion both are spent,
Twining clean away.

Is the person empty air,
Is the spectre clay,
That love, lent substance by despair,
Wanes and leaves you lonely there
On the bridal day?

FULL MOON

As I walked out that sultry night,
  I heard the stroke of One.
The moon, attained to her full height,
  Stood beaming like the sun:
She exorcized the ghostly wheat
To mute assent in love's defeat,
  Whose tryst had now begun.

The fields lay sick beneath my tread,
  A tedious owlet cried,
A nightingale above my head
  With this or that replied—
Like man and wife who nightly keep
Inconsequent debate in sleep
  As they dream side by side.

Your phantom wore the moon's cold mask,
  My phantom wore the same;
Forgetful of a feverish task
  In hope of which they came,
Each image held the other's eyes
And watched a grey distraction rise
  To cloud the eager flame—

To cloud the eager flame of love,
  To fog the shining gate;
They held the tyrannous queen above
  Sole mover of their fate;
They glared as marble statues glare
Across the tessellated stair
  Or down the halls of state.

And now warm earth was Arctic sea,
  Each breath came dagger-keen;
Two bergs of glinting ice were we,
  The broad moon sailed between;
There swam the mermaids, tailed and finned,
And love went by upon the wind
  As though it had not been.

VANITY

Be assured, the Dragon is not dead
But once more from the pools of peace
Shall rear his fabulous green head.

The flowers of innocence shall cease
And like a harp the wind shall roar
And the clouds shake an angry fleece.

'Here, here is certitude,' you swore,
'Below this lightning-blasted tree.
Where once it struck, it strikes no more.

'Two lovers in one house agree.
The roof is tight, the walls unshaken.
As now, so must it always be.'

Such prophecies of joy awaken
The toad who dreams away the past
Under your hearth-stone, light-forsaken,

Who knows that certitude at last
Must melt away in vanity—
No gate is fast, no door is fast—

That thunder bursts from the blue sky,
That gardens of the mind fall waste,
That fountains of the heart run dry.

PURE DEATH

We looked, we loved, and therewith instantly
Death became terrible to you and me.
By love we disenthralled our natural terror
From every comfortable philosopher
Or tall, grey doctor of divinity:
Death stood at last in his true rank and order.

It happened soon, so wild of heart were we,
Exchange of gifts grew to a malady:
Their worth rose always higher on each side
Till there seemed nothing but ungivable pride
That yet remained ungiven, and this degree
Called a conclusion not to be denied.

Then we at last bethought ourselves, made shift
And simultaneously this final gift
Gave: each with shaking hands unlocks
The sinister, long, brass-bound coffin-box,
Unwraps pure death, with such bewilderment
As greeted our love's first acknowledgement.

SICK LOVE

O Love, be fed with apples while you may,
And feel the sun and ride in royal array,
A smiling innocent on the heavenly causeway,

Though in what listening horror for the cry
That soars in outer blackness dismally,
The dumb blind beast, the paranoiac fury,

Be warm, enjoy the season, lift your head,
Exquisite in the pulse of tainted blood,
That shivering glory not to be despised.

Take your delight in momentariness,
Walk between dark and dark—a shining space
With the grave's narrowness, though not its peace.

ULYSSES

To the much-tossed Ulysses, never done
  With woman whether gowned as wife or whore,
Penelope and Circe seemed as one:
She like a whore made his lewd fancies run,
  And wifely she a hero to him bore.

Their counter-changings terrified his way:
  They were the clashing rocks, Symplegades.
Scylla and Charybdis too were they;
Now angry storms frosting the sea with spray
  And now the lotus island's drunken ease.

They multiplied into the Sirens' throng,
  Forewarned by fear of whom he stood bound fast
Hand and foot helpless to the vessel's mast,
Yet would not stop his ears: daring the song
  He groaned and sweated till their shore was past.

One, two and many. Flesh had made him blind,
  Flesh had one pleasure only in the act,
Flesh set one purpose only in the mind:
Triumph of flesh and afterwards to find
  Still those same terrors wherewith flesh was racked.

His wiles were witty and his fame far known,
Every king's daughter sought him for her own,
  Yet he was nothing to be won or lost.
  All lands to him were Ithaca; love-tossed
He loathed the fraud, yet would not bed alone.

THE SUCCUBUS

Thus will despair
In ecstasy of nightmare
Fetch you a devil-woman through the air,
   To slide below the sweated sheet
And kiss your lips in answer to your prayer
   And lock her hands with yours and your feet with her feet.

Yet why does she
Come never as longed-for beauty
Slender and cool, with limbs lovely to see,
   (The bedside candle guttering high)
And toss her head so the thick curls fall free
   Of halo'd breast, firm belly and long, slender thigh?

Why with hot face,
With paunched and uddered carcase,
Sudden and greedily does she embrace,
   Gulping away your soul, she lies so close,
Fathering brats on you of her own race?
   Yet is the fancy grosser than your lusts were gross?

THE CHRISTMAS ROBIN

The snows of February had buried Christmas
Deep in the woods, where grew self-seeded
The fir-trees of a Christmas yet unknown,
Without a candle or a strand of tinsel.

Nevertheless when, hand in hand, plodding
Between the frozen ruts, we lovers paused
And 'Christmas trees!' cried suddenly together,
Christmas was there again, as in December.

We velveted our love with fantasy
Down a long vista-row of Christmas trees,
Whose coloured candles slowly guttered down
As grandchildren came trooping round our knees.

But he knew better, did the Christmas robin—
The murderous robin with his breast aglow
And legs apart, in a spade-handle perched:
He prophesied more snow, and worse than snow.

FACT OF THE ACT

On the other side of the world's narrow lane
You lie in bed, your young breasts tingling
With imagined kisses, your lips puckered,
Your fists tight.

Dreaming yourself naked in my arms,
Free from discovery, under our oak;
The high sun peering through thick branches,
All winds mute.

Endlessly you prolong the moment
Of your delirium: a first engagement,
Silent, inevitable, fearful,
Honey-sweet.

Will it be so in fact? Will fact mirror
Your virginal ecstasies:
True love, uncircumstantial,
No blame, no shame?

It is for you, now, to say 'come';
It is for you, now, to prepare the bed;
It is for you as the sole hostess
Of your white dreams—

It is for you to open the locked gate,
It is for you to shake ripe apples down,
It is for you to halve them with your hands
That both may eat.

Yet expectation lies as far from fact
As fact's own after-glow in memory;
Fact is a dark return to man's beginnings,
Test of our hardihood, test of a wilful
And blind acceptance of each other
As also flesh.

AT FIRST SIGHT

'Love at first sight,' some say, misnaming
Discovery of twinned helplessness
Against the huge tug of procreation.

But friendship at first sight? This also
Catches fiercely at the surprised heart
So that the cheek blanches and then blushes.

DOWN, WANTON, DOWN!

Down, wanton, down! Have you no shame
That at the whisper of Love's name,
Or Beauty's, presto! up you raise
Your angry head and stand at gaze?

Poor bombard-captain, sworn to reach
The ravelin and effect a breach—
Indifferent what you storm or why,
So be that in the breach you die!

Love may be blind, but Love at least
Knows what is man and what mere beast;
Or Beauty wayward, but requires
True delicacy from her squires.

Tell me, my witless, whose one boast
Could be your staunchness at the post,
When were you made a man of parts
To think fine and profess the arts?

Will many-gifted Beauty come
Bowing to your bald rule of thumb,
Or Love swear loyalty to your crown?
Be gone, have done! Down, wanton, down!

NEVER SUCH LOVE

Twined together and, as is customary,
For words of rapture groping, they
'Never such love,' swore, 'ever before was!'
Contrast with all loves that had failed or staled
Registered their own as love indeed.

But was this not to blab idly
The heart's fated inconstancy?
Better in love to seal the love-sure lips,
For truly love was before words were,
And: no word given, no word broken.

When the name 'love' is uttered
(Love, the near-honourable malady
With which in greed and haste they
Each other do infect and curse)
Or, worse, is written down. . . .

Wise after the event, by love withered,
A 'never more!' most frantically
Sorrow and shame would proclaim
Such as, they'd swear, never before were:
True lovers even in this.

A JEALOUS MAN

To be homeless is a pride
To the jealous man prowling
Hungry down the night lanes,

Who has no steel at his side,
No drink hot in his mouth,
But a mind dream-enlarged,

Who witnesses warfare,
Man with woman, hugely
Raging from hedge to hedge:

The raw knotted oak-club
Clenched in the raw fist,
The ivy-noose well flung,

The thronged din of battle,
Gaspings of the throat-snared,
Snores of the battered dying,

Tall corpses, braced together,
Fallen in clammy furrows,
Male and female,

Or, among haulms of nettle
Humped, in noisome heaps,
Male and female.

(Here, the rain-worn headstone,
There, the Celtic cross
In rank white marble.)

This jealous man is smitten,
His fear-jerked forehead
Sweats a fine musk;

A score of bats bewitched
By the ruttish odour
Swoop singing at his head;

Nuns bricked up alive
Within the neighbouring wall
Wail in cat-like longing.

Crow, cocks, crow loud,
Reprieve the doomed devil—
Has he not died enough?

Now, out of careless sleep,
She wakes and greets him coldly,
The woman at home,

She, with a private wonder
At shoes bemired and bloody—
His war was not hers.

THE FOREBODING

Looking by chance in at the open window
  I saw my own self seated in his chair
With gaze abstracted, furrowed forehead,
  Unkempt hair.

I thought that I had suddenly come to die,
  That to a cold corpse this was my farewell,
Until the pen moved slowly upon paper
  And tears fell.

He had written a name, yours, in printed letters:
  One word on which bemusedly to pore—
No protest, no desire, your naked name,
  Nothing more.

Would it be tomorrow, would it be next year?
  But the vision was not false, this much I knew;
And I turned angrily from the open window
  Aghast at you.

Why never a warning, either by speech or look,
  That the love you cruelly gave me could not last?
Already it was too late: the bait swallowed,
  The hook fast.

WITH HER LIPS ONLY

This honest wife, challenged at dusk
At the garden gate, under a rising moon,
In scent of honeysuckle, dared to deny
Love to an urgent lover: with her lips only,
Not with her heart. It was no assignation.
Taken aback, what could she say else?
For the children's sake, the lie was venial;
'For the children's sake', she argued with her conscience.

Yet a mortal lie must follow before dawn:
Challenged as usual in her own bed,
She protests love to an urgent husband,
Not with her heart but with her lips only;
'For the children's sake', she argues with her conscience,
'For the children'—turning suddenly cold towards them.

Part 2

ON PORTENTS

If strange things happen where she is,
So that men say that graves open
And the dead walk, or that futurity
Opens its womb and the unborn are shed,
Such portents are not to be wondered at,
Being tourbillions in Time made
By the strong pulling of her bladed mind
Through that ever-reluctant element.

THE TERRACED VALLEY

In a deep thought of you and concentration
I came by hazard to a new region:
The unnecessary sun was not there,
The necessary earth lay without care—
For more than sunshine warmed the skin
Of the round world that was turned outside-in.

Calm sea beyond the terraced valley
Without horizon easily was spread,
As it were overhead,
Washing the mountain-spurs behind me;
The unnecessary sky was not there,
Therefore no heights, no deeps, no birds of the air.

Neat outside-inside, neat below-above,
Hermaphrodizing love.
Neat this-way-that-way and without mistake:
On the right hand could slide the left glove.
Neat over-under: the young snake
Through an unyielding shell his path could break.
Singing of kettles, like a singing brook,
Made out-of-doors a fireside nook.

But you, my love, where had you then your station?
Seeing that on this counter-earth together
We go not distant from each other;
I knew you near me in that strange region,
So searched for you, in hope to see you stand
On some near olive-terrace, in the heat,
The left-hand glove drawn on your right hand,
The empty snake's egg perfect at your feet—

But found you nowhere in the wide land,
And cried disconsolately, until you spoke
Immediate at my elbow, and your voice broke
This trick of time, changing the world about
To once more inside-in and outside-out.

LIKE SNOW

She, then, like snow in a dark night,
Fell secretly. And the world waked
With dazzling of the drowsy eye,
So that some muttered 'Too much light'
And drew the curtains close.
Like snow, warmer than fingers feared,
Though to soil friendly;
Holding the histories of the night
In yet unmelted tracks.

END OF PLAY

We have reached the end of pastime, for always,
Ourselves and everyone, though few confess it
Or see the sky other than, as of old,
A foolish-smiling Mary-mantle blue;

Though life may still seem to dawdle golden
In some June landscape among giant flowers,
The grass to shine as cruelly green as ever,
Faith to descend in a chariot from the sky . . .

May seem only: a mirror and an echo
Mediate henceforth with vision and sound.
The cry of faith, no longer mettlesome,
Sounds as a blind man's pitiful plea of 'blind'.

We have at last ceased idling, which to regret
Were as shallow as to ask our milk-teeth back;
As many forthwith do, and on their knees
Call lugubriously upon chaste Christ.

We tell no lies now, at last cannot be
The rogues we were—so evilly linked in sense
With what we scrutinized that lion or tiger
Could leap from every copse, strike and devour us.

No more shall love in hypocritic pomp
Conduct its innocents through a dance of shame,
From timid touching of gloved fingers
To frantic laceration of naked breasts.

Yet love survives, the word carved on a sill
Under antique dread of the headsman's axe;
It is the echoing mind, as in the mirror
We stare on our dazed trunks at the block kneeling.

A LOVE STORY

The full moon easterly rising, furious,
Against a winter sky ragged with red;
The hedges high in snow, the owls raving—
Solemnities not easy to withstand:
A shiver wakes the spine.

In boyhood, having encountered the scene,
I suffered horror. I fetched the moon home,
With owls and snow, to nurse in my head
Throughout the trials of a new Spring,
Famine unassuaged.

But fell in love, and made a lodgement
Of love on those chill ramparts.
Her image was my ensign: snows melted,
Hedges sprouted, the moon tenderly shone,
The owls trilled with tongues of nightingale.

These were all lies, though they matched the time,
And brought me less than luck: her image
Warped in the weather, turned beldamish.
Then back came winter on me at a bound,
The pallid sky heaved with a moon-quake.

Dangerous it had been with love-notes
To serenade Queen Famine.
In tears I recomposed the former scene,
Let the snow lie, watched the moon rise, suffered the owls,
Paid homage to them of unevent.

DAWN BOMBARDMENT

Guns from the sea open against us:
The smoke rocks bodily in the casemate
And a yell of doom goes up.
We count and bless each new, heavy concussion—
Captives awaiting rescue.

Visiting angel of the wild-fire hair
Who in dream reassured us nightly
Where we lay fettered,
Laugh at us, as we wake—our faces
So tense with hope the tears run down.

THE THIEVES

Lovers in the act dispense
With such meum-tuum sense
As might warningly reveal
What they must not pick or steal,
And their nostrum is to say:
'I and you are both away.'

After, when they disentwine
You from me and yours from mine,
Neither can be certain who
Was that I whose mine was you.
To the act again they go
More completely not to know.

Theft is theft and raid is raid
Though reciprocally made.
Lovers, the conclusion is
Doubled sighs and jealousies
In a single heart that grieves
For lost honour among thieves.

TO SLEEP

The mind's eye sees as the heart mirrors:
Loving in part, I did not see you whole,
Grew flesh-enraged that I could not conjure
A whole you to attend my fever-fit
In the doubtful hour between a night and day
And be Sleep that had kept so long away.

Of you sometimes a hand, a brooch, a shoe
Wavered beside me, unarticulated—
As the vexed insomniac dream-forges;
And the words I chose for your voice to speak
Echoed my own voice with its dry creak.

Now that I love you, now that I recall
All scattered elements of will that swooped
By night as jealous dreams through windows
To circle above the beds like bats,
Or as dawn-birds flew blindly at the panes
In curiosity rattling out their brains—

Now that I love you, as not before,
Now that you speak and are, as not before:
The mind clears and the heart true-mirrors you
Where at my side an early watch you keep
And all self-bruising heads loll into sleep.

THE OATH

The doubt and the passion
Falling away from them,
　In that instant both
Take timely courage
From the sky's clearness
　To confirm an oath.

Her loves are his loves,
His trust is her trust;
　Else all were grief
And they, lost ciphers
On a yellowing page,
　Death overleaf.

Rumour of old battle
Growls across the air;
　Then let it growl
With no more terror
Than the creaking stair
　Or the calling owl.

She knows, as he knows,
Of a faithful-always
　And an always-dear
By early emblems
Prognosticated,
　Fulfilled here.

MID-WINTER WAKING

Stirring suddenly from long hibernation,
I knew myself once more a poet
Guarded by timeless principalities
Against the worm of death, this hillside haunting;
And presently dared open both my eyes.

O gracious, lofty, shone against from under,
Back-of-the-mind-far clouds like towers;
And you, sudden warm airs that blow
Before the expected season of new blossom,
While sheep still gnaw at roots and lambless go—

Be witness that on waking, this mid-winter,
I found her hand in mine laid closely
Who shall watch out the Spring with me.
We stared in silence all around us
But found no winter anywhere to see.

THE DOOR

When she came suddenly in
It seemed the door could never close again,
Nor even did she close it—she, she—
The room lay open to a visiting sea
Which no door could restrain.

Yet when at last she smiled, tilting her head
To take her leave of me,
Where she had smiled, instead
There was a dark door closing endlessly,
The waves receded.

THROUGH NIGHTMARE

Never be disenchanted of
That place you sometimes dream yourself into,
Lying at large remove beyond all dream,
Or those you find there, though but seldom
In their company seated—

The untameable, the live, the gentle.
Have you not known them? Whom? They carry
Time looped so river-wise about their house
There's no way in by history's road
To name or number them.

In your sleepy eyes I read the journey
Of which disjointedly you tell; which stirs
My loving admiration, that you should travel
Through nightmare to a lost and moated land,
Who are timorous by nature.

SHE TELLS HER LOVE WHILE HALF ASLEEP

She tells her love while half asleep,
    In the dark hours,
        With half-words whispered low:
As Earth stirs in her winter sleep
    And puts out grass and flowers,
        Despite the snow,
        Despite the falling snow.

THESEUS AND ARIADNE

High on his figured couch beyond the waves
He dreams, in dream recalling her set walk
Down paths of oyster-shell bordered with flowers,
Across the shadowy turf below the vines.
He sighs: 'Deep sunk in my erroneous past
She haunts those ruins and those ravaged lawns.'

Yet still unharmed it stands, the regal house
Crooked with age and overtopped by pines
Where first he wearied of her constancy;
And with a surer foot she goes than when
Dread of his hate was thunder in the air,
When the pines agonized with flaws of wind
And flowers glared up at her with frantic eyes.
Of him, now all is done, she never dreams
But calls a living blessing down upon
What he supposes rubble and rank grass;
Playing the queen to nobler company.

TO JUAN AT THE WINTER SOLSTICE

There is one story and one story only
That will prove worth your telling,
Whether as learned bard or gifted child;
To it all lines or lesser gauds belong
That startle with their shining
Such common stories as they stray into.

Is it of trees you tell, their months and virtues,
Or strange beasts that beset you,
Of birds that croak at you the Triple will?
Or of the Zodiac and how slow it turns
Below the Boreal Crown,
Prison of all true kings that ever reigned?

Water to water, ark again to ark,
From woman back to woman:
So each new victim treads unfalteringly
The never altered circuit of his fate,
Bringing twelve peers as witness
Both to his starry rise and starry fall.

Or is it of the Virgin's silver beauty,
All fish below the thighs?
She in her left hand bears a leafy quince;
When with her right she crooks a finger, smiling,
How may the King hold back?
Royally then he barters life for love.

Or of the undying snake from chaos hatched,
Whose coils contain the ocean,
Into whose chops with naked sword he springs,
Then in black water, tangled by the reeds,
Battles three days and nights,
To be spewed up beside her scalloped shore?

Much snow is falling, winds roar hollowly,
The owl hoots from the elder,
Fear in your heart cries to the loving-cup:
Sorrow to sorrow as the sparks fly upward.
The log groans and confesses:
There is one story and one story only.

Dwell on her graciousness, dwell on her smiling,
Do not forget what flowers
The great boar trampled down in ivy time.
Her brow was creamy as the crested wave,
Her sea-grey eyes were wild
But nothing promised that is not performed.

TO BE CALLED A BEAR

Bears gash the forest trees
  To mark the bounds
  Of their own hunting grounds;
They follow the wild bees
  Point by point home
  For love of honeycomb;
They browse on blueberries.

Then should I stare
If I am called a bear,
And it is not the truth?
Unkempt and surly with a sweet tooth
I tilt my muzzle toward the starry hub
Where Queen Callisto guards her cub;

But envy those that here
  All winter breathing slow
  Sleep warm under the snow,
That yawn awake when the skies clear,
  And lank with longing grow
No more than one brief month a year.

BEAUTY IN TROUBLE

Beauty in trouble flees to the good angel
  On whom she can rely
To pay her cab-fare, run a steaming bath,
  Poultice her bruised eye;

Will not at first, whether for shame or caution,
  Her difficulty disclose;
Until he draws a cheque-book from his plumage,
  Asking how much she owes.

(Breakfast in bed: coffee and marmalade,
  Toast, eggs, orange-juice,
After a long, sound sleep—the first since when?—
  And no word of abuse.)

Loves him less only than her saint-like mother,
  Promises to repay
His loans and most seraphic thoughtfulness
  A million-fold one day.

Beauty grows plump, renews her broken courage
  And, borrowing ink and pen,
Writes a news-letter to the evil angel
  (Her first gay act since when?):

The fiend who beats, betrays and sponges on her,
  Persuades her white is black,
Flaunts vespertilian wing and cloven hoof;
  And soon will fetch her back.

Virtue, good angel, is its own reward:
  Your guineas were well spent.
But would you to the marriage of true minds
  Admit impediment?

THE SONG OF BLODEUWEDD

[Reassembled from the deliberately confused mediaeval poem medley,
Câd Goddeu, in the *Red Book of Hergest*, hitherto regarded as nonsensical.]

Not of father nor of mother
Was my blood, was my body.
I was spellbound by Gwydion,
Prime enchanter of the Britons,
When he formed me from nine blossoms,
   Nine buds of various kind:
From primrose of the mountain,
Broom, meadow-street and cockle,
   Together intertwined,
From the bean in its shade bearing
A white spectral army
   Of earth, of earthy kind,
From blossoms of the nettle,
Oak, thorn and bashful chestnut—
Nine powers of nine flowers,
   Nine powers in me combined,
     Nine buds of plant and tree.
Long and white are my fingers
     As the ninth wave of the sea.

LAMENT FOR PASIPHAË

Dying Sun, shine warm a little longer!
My eye, dazzled with tears, shall dazzle yours,
Conjuring you to shine and not to move.
You, Sun, and I all afternoon have laboured
Beneath a dewless and oppressive cloud—
A fleece now gilded with our common grief
That this must be a night without a moon.
Dying Sun, shine warm a little longer!

Faithless she was not: she was very woman,
Smiling with dire impartiality,
Sovereign, with heart unmatched, adored of men,
Until Spring's cuckoo with bedraggled plumes
Tempted her pity and our truth betrayed.
Then she who shone for all resigned her being,
And this must be a night without a moon.
Dying Sun, shine warm a little longer!

COUNTING THE BEATS

You, love, and I,
(He whispers) you and I,
And if no more than only you and I
What care you or I?

Counting the beats,
Counting the slow heart beats,
The bleeding to death of time in slow heart beats,
Wakeful they lie.

Cloudless day,
Night, and a cloudless day,
Yet the huge storm will burst upon their heads one day
From a bitter sky.

Where shall we be,
(She whispers) where shall we be,
When death strikes home, O where then shall we be
Who were you and I?

Not there but here,
(He whispers) only here,
As we are, here, together, now and here,
Always you and I.

Counting the beats,
Counting the slow heart beats,
The bleeding to death of time in slow heart beats,
Wakeful they lie.

THE YOUNG CORDWAINER

SHE: Love, why have you led me here
    To this lampless hall,
  A place of despair and fear
    Where blind things crawl?

HE: Not I, but your complaint
    Heard by the riverside
  That primrose scent grew faint
    And desire died.

SHE: Kisses had lost virtue
    As yourself must know;
  I declared what, alas, was true
    And still shall do so.

HE: Mount, sweetheart, this main stair
    Where bandogs at the foot
  Their crooked gilt teeth bare
    Between jaws of soot.

SHE: I loathe them, how they stand
    Like prick-eared spies.
  Hold me fast by the left hand;
    I walk with closed eyes.

HE: Primrose has periwinkle
    As her mortal fellow:
  Five leaves, blue and baleful,
    Five of true yellow.

SHE: Overhead, what's overhead?
    Where would you take me?
  My feet stumble for dread,
    My wits forsake me.

HE: Flight on flight, floor above floor,
    In suspense of doom
  To a locked secret door
    And a white-walled room.

SHE: Love, have you the pass-word,
    Or have you the key,
  With the sharp naked sword
    And wine to revive me?

HE: Enter: here is starlight,
    Here the state bed
  Where your man lies all night
    With blue flowers garlanded.

SHE: Ah, the cool, open window
    Of this confessional!
  With wine at my elbow,
  And sword beneath the pillow,
    I shall perfect all.

THE SURVIVOR

To die with a forlorn hope, but soon to be raised
By hags, the spoilers of the field, to elude their claws
And stand once more on a well-swept parade-ground,
Scarred and bemedalled, sword upright in fist
At head of a new undaunted company . . .

Is this joy: to be doubtless alive again,
And the others dead? Will your nostrils gladly savour
The fragrance, always new, of a first hedge-rose?
Will your ears be charmed by the thrush's melody
Sung as though he had himself devised it?

And is this joy: after the double suicide
(Heart against heart) to be restored entire,
To smooth your hair and wash away the life-blood,
And presently seek a young and innocent bride,
Whispering in the dark: 'for ever and ever'?

Part 3

QUESTIONS IN A WOOD

The parson to his pallid spouse,
  The hangman to his whore,
Do both not mumble the same vows,
  Both knock at the same door?

And when the fury of their knocks
  Has waned, and that was that,
What answer comes, unless the pox
  Or one more parson's brat?

Tell me, my love, my flower of flowers,
  True woman to this man,
What have their deeds to do with ours
  Or any we might plan?

Your startled gaze, your restless hand,
  Your hair like Thames in flood,
And choked voice, battling to command
  The insurgence of your blood:

How can they spell the dark word said
  Ten thousand times a night
By women as corrupt and dead
  As you are proud and bright?

And how can I, in the same breath,
  Though warned against the cheat,
Vilely deliver love to death
  Wrapped in a rumpled sheet?
Yet, if from delicacy of pride
  We choose to hold apart,
Will no blue hag appear to ride
  Hell's wager in each heart?

THE PORTRAIT

She speaks always in her own voice
Even to strangers; but those other women
Exercise their borrowed, or false, voices
Even on sons and daughters.

She can walk invisibly at noon
Along the high road; but those other women
Gleam phosphorescent—broad hips and gross fingers—
Down every lampless alley.

She is wild and innocent, pledged to love
Through all disaster; but those other women
Decry her for a witch or a common drab
And glare back when she greets them.

Here is her portrait, gazing sidelong at me,
The hair in disarray, the young eyes pleading:
'And you, love? As unlike those other men
As I those other women?'

THE STRAW

Peace, the wild valley streaked with torrents,
A hoopoe perched on his warm rock. Then why
This tremor of the straw between my fingers?

What should I fear? Have I not testimony
In her own hand, signed with her own name
That my love fell as lightning on her heart?

These questions, bird, are not rhetorical.
Watch how the straw twitches and leaps
As though the earth quaked at a distance.

Requited love; but better unrequited
If this chance instrument gives warning
Of cataclysmic anguish far away.

Were she at ease, warmed by the thought of me,
Would not my hand stay steady as this rock?
Have I undone her by my vehemence?

HERCULES AT NEMEA

Muse, you have bitten through my fool's-finger.
Fierce as a lioness you seized it
In your white teeth most amorously;
And I stared back, dauntless and fiery-eyed,
Challenging you to maim me for my pride.

See me a fulvous hero of nine fingers—
Sufficient grasp for bow and arrow.
My beard bristles in exultation:
Let all Nemea look and understand
Why you have set your mark on this right hand.

DIALOGUE ON THE HEADLAND

SHE: You'll not forget these rocks and what I told you?
HE: How could I? Never: whatever happens.
SHE: What do you think might happen?
    Might you fall out of love?—did you mean that?
HE: Never, never! 'Whatever' was a sop
    For jealous listeners in the shadows.
SHE: You haven't answered me. I asked:
    'What do you think might happen?'
HE: Whatever happens: though the skies should fall
    Raining their larks and vultures in our laps—
SHE: 'Though the seas turn to slime'—say that—
    'Though water-snakes be hatched with six heads.'
HE: Though the seas turn to slime, or tower
    In an arching wave above us, three miles high—
SHE: 'Though she should break with you'—dare you say that?—
    'Though she deny her words on oath.'
HE: I had that in my mind to say, or nearly;
    It hurt so much I choked it back.
SHE: How many other days can't you forget?
    How many other loves and landscapes?
HE: You are jealous?
SHE: Damnably.
HE: The past is past.
SHE: And this?
HE: Whatever happens, this goes on.
SHE: Without a future? Sweetheart, tell me now:
    What do you want of me? I must know that.
HE: Nothing that isn't freely mine already.
SHE: Say what is freely yours and you shall have it.
HE: Nothing that, loving you, I could dare take.
SHE: O, for an answer with no 'nothing' in it!
HE: Then give me everything that's left.
SHE: Left after what?
HE: After whatever happens:
    Skies have already fallen, seas are slime,
    Watersnakes poke and peer six-headedly—
SHE: And I lie snugly in the Devil's arms.
HE: I said: 'Whatever happens.' Are you crying?
SHE: You'll not forget me—ever, ever, ever?

CAT-GODDESSES

A perverse habit of cat-goddesses—
Even the blackest of them, black as coals
Save for a new moon blazing on each breast,
With coral tongues and beryl eyes like lamps,
Long-leggèd, pacing three by three in nines—
This obstinate habit is to yield themselves,
In verisimilar love-ecstasies,
To tatter-eared and slinking alley-toms
No less below the common run of cats
Than they above it; which they do for spite,
To provoke jealousy—not the least abashed
By such gross-headed, rabbit-coloured litters
As soon they shall be happy to desert.

THE BLUE-FLY

Five summer days, five summer nights,
The ignorant, loutish, giddy blue-fly
Hung without motion on the cling peach,
Humming occasionally: 'O my love, my fair one!'
    As in the *Canticles*.

Magnified one thousand times, the insect
Looks farcically human; laugh if you will!
Bald head, stage-fairy wings, blear eyes,
A caved-in chest, hairy black mandibles,
    Long spindly thighs.

The crime was detected on the sixth day.
What then could be said or done? By anyone?
It would have been vindictive, mean and what-not
To swat that fly for being a blue-fly,
    For debauch of a peach.

Is it fair, either, to bring a microscope
To bear on the case, even in search of truth?
Nature, doubtless, has some compelling cause
To glut the carriers of her epidemics—
    Nor did the peach complain.

A LOST JEWEL

Who on your breast pillows his head now,
Jubilant to have won
The heart beneath on fire for him alone,

At dawn will hear you, plagued by nightmare,
Mumble and weep
About some blue jewel you were sworn to keep.

Wake, blink, laugh out in reassurance,
Yet your tears will say:
'It was not mine to lose or give away.

'For love it shone—never for the madness
Of a strange bed—
Light on my finger, fortune in my head.'

Roused by your naked grief and beauty,
For lust he will burn:
'Turn to me, sweetheart! Why do you not turn?'

THE WINDOW SILL

Presage and caveat not only seem
To come in dream,
But do so come in dream.

When the cock crew and phantoms floated by,
This dreamer I
Out of the house went I,

Down long unsteady streets to a queer square;
And who was there,
Or whom did I know there?

Julia, leaning on her window sill.
'I love you still,'
She said, 'O love me still!'

I answered: 'Julia, do you love me best?'
'What of this breast,'
She mourned, 'this flowery breast?'

Then a wild sobbing spread from door to door,
And every floor
Cried shame on every floor,

As she unlaced her bosom to disclose
Each breast a rose,
A white and cankered rose.

SPOILS

When all is over and you march for home,
The spoils of war are easily disposed of:
Standards, weapons of combat, helmets, drums
May decorate a staircase or a study,
While lesser gleanings of the battlefield—
Coins, watches, wedding-rings, gold teeth and such—
Are sold anonymously for solid cash.

The spoils of love present a different case.
When all is over and you march for home:
That lock of hair, these letters and the portrait
May not be publicly displayed; nor sold;
Nor burned; nor returned (the heart being obstinate)—
Yet never dare entrust them to a safe
For fear they burn a hole through two-foot steel.

RHEA

On her shut lids the lightning flickers,
Thunder explodes above her bed,
An inch from her lax arm the rain hisses;
Discrete she lies,

Not dead but entranced, dreamlessly
With slow breathing, her lips curved
In a half-smile archaic, her breast bare,
Hair astream.

The house rocks, a flood suddenly rising
Bears away bridges: oak and ash
Are shivered to the roots—royal green timber.
She nothing cares.

(Divine Augustus, trembling at the storm,
Wrapped sealskin on his thumb; divine Gaius
Made haste to hide himself in a deep cellar,
Distraught by fear.)

Rain, thunder, lightning: pretty children.
'Let them play,' her mother-mind repeats;
'They do no harm, unless from high spirits
Or by mishap.'

THE FACE IN THE MIRROR

Grey haunted eyes, absent-mindedly glaring
From wide, uneven orbits; one brow drooping
Somewhat over the eye
Because of a missile fragment still inhering,
Skin deep, as a foolish record of old-world fighting.

Crookedly broken nose—low tackling caused it;
Cheeks, furrowed; coarse grey hair, flying frenetic;
Forehead, wrinkled and high;
Jowls, prominent; ears, large; jaw, pugilistic;
Teeth, few; lips, full and ruddy; mouth, ascetic.

I pause with razor poised, scowling derision
At the mirrored man whose beard needs my attention,
And once more ask him why
He still stands ready, with a boy's presumption,
To court the queen in her high silk pavilion.

FORBIDDEN WORDS

There are some words carry a curse with them:
Smooth-trodden, abstract, slippery vocables.
They beckon like a path of stepping stones;
But lift them up and watch what writhes or scurries!

Concepts barred from the close language of love—
Darling, you use no single word of the list,
Unless ironically in truth's defence
To volley it back against the abstractionist.

Which is among your several holds on my heart;
For you are no uninstructed child of Nature,
But passed in schools and attained the laurel wreath—
Only to trample it on Apollo's floor.

POSSIBLY

Possibly is not a monosyllable;
   Then answer me
At once if possible
   Monosyllabically,
No will be good, *Yes* even better
Though longer by one letter.

Possibly is not a monosyllable,
   And my heart flies shut
At the warning rumble
   Of a suspended *But* . . .
O love, be brief and exact
In confession of simple fact!

A SLICE OF WEDDING CAKE

Why have such scores of lovely, gifted girls
  Married impossible men?
Simple self-sacrifice may be ruled out,
  And missionary endeavour, nine times out of ten.

Repeat 'impossible men': not merely rustic,
  Foul-tempered or depraved
(Dramatic foils chosen to show the world
  How well women behave, and always have behaved).

Impossible men: idle, illiterate,
  Self-pitying, dirty, sly,
For whose appearance even in City parks
  Excuses must be made to casual passers-by.

Has God's supply of tolerable husbands
  Fallen, in fact, so low?
Or do I always over-value woman
  At the expense of man?
                    Do I?
                        It might be so.

CALL IT A GOOD MARRIAGE

Call it a good marriage—
For no one ever questioned
Her warmth, his masculinity,
Their interlocking views;
Except one stray graphologist
Who frowned in speculation
At her h's and her s's,
His p's and w's.

Though few would still subscribe
To the monogamic axiom
That strife below the hip-bones
Need not estrange the heart,
Call it a good marriage:
More drew those two together,
Despite a lack of children,
Than pulled them apart.

Call it a good marriage:
They never fought in public,
They acted circumspectly
And faced the world with pride;
Thus the hazards of their love-bed
Were none of our damned business—
Till as jurymen we sat upon
Two deaths by suicide.

AROUND THE MOUNTAIN

Some of you may know, others perhaps can guess
  How it is to walk all night through summer rain
(Thin rain that shrouds a beneficent full moon),
  To circle a mountain, and then limp home again.

The experience varies with a traveller's age
  And bodily strength, and strength of the love affair
That harries him out of doors in steady drizzle,
  With neither jacket nor hat, and holds him there.

Still, let us concede some common elements:
  Wild-fire that, until midnight, burns his feet;
And surging rankly up, strong on the palate,
  Scents of July, imprisoned by long heat.

Add: the sub-human, black tree-silhouettes
  Against a featureless pale pall of sky;
Unseen, gurgling water; the bulk and menace
  Of haunted houses; a wraith wandering by.

Milestones, each one witness of a new mood—
  Anger, desperation, grief, regret;
Her too-familiar face that whirls and totters
  In memory, never willing to stay set.

Whoever makes the desired turning-point,
  Which means another fifteen miles to go,
Learns more from dawn than love, so far, has taught him:
  Especially the false dawn, when cocks first crow.

Those last few miles are easy: being assured
  Of the truth, why should he fabricate fresh lies?
His house looms up; the eaves drip drowsily;
  The windows blaze to a resolute sunrise.

Part 4

LYCEIA

All the wolves of the forest
Howl for Lyceia,
Crowding together
In a close circle,
Tongues a-loll.

A silver serpent
Coiled at her waist
And a quiver at knee,
She combs fine tresses
With a fine comb:

Wolf-like, woman-like,
Gazing about her,
Greeting the wolves;
Partial to many,
Yet masked in pride.

The young wolves snarl,
They snap at one another
Under the moon.
'Beasts, be reasonable,
My beauty is my own!'

Lyceia has a light foot
For a weaving walk.
Her archer muscles
Warn them how tightly
She can stretch the string.

I question Lyceia,
Whom I find posted
Under the pine trees
One early morning:
'What do the wolves learn?'

'They learn only envy,'
Lyceia answers,
'Envy and hope.
Hope and chagrin.
Would you howl too
In that wolfish circle?'
She laughs as she speaks.

SYMPTOMS OF LOVE

Love is a universal migraine,
A bright stain on the vision
Blotting out reason.

Symptoms of true love
Are leanness, jealousy,
Laggard dawns;

Are omens and nightmares—
Listening for a knock,
Waiting for a sign:

For a touch of her fingers
In a darkened room,
For a searching look.

Take courage, lover!
Could you endure such grief
At any hand but hers?

THE SHARP RIDGE

Since now I dare not ask
Any gift from you, or gentle task,
Or lover's promise—nor yet refuse
Whatever I can give and you dare choose—
Have pity on us both: choose well
On this sharp ridge dividing death from hell.

UNDER THE OLIVES

We never would have loved had love not struck
Swifter than reason, and despite reason:
Under the olives, our hands interlocked,
We both fell silent:
Each listened for the other's answering
Sigh of unreasonableness—
Innocent, gentle, bold, enduring, proud.

THE VISITATION

Drowsing in my chair of disbelief
I watch the door as it slowly opens—
A trick of the night wind?

Your slender body seems a shaft of moonlight
Against the door as it gently closes.
Do you cast no shadow?

Your whisper is too soft for credence,
Your tread like blossom drifting from a bough,
Your touch even softer.

You wear that sorrowful and tender mask
Which on high mountain tops in heather-flow
Entrances lonely shepherds;

And though a single word scatters all doubts
I quake for wonder at your choice of me:
Why, why and why?

FRAGMENT

Are you shaken, are you stirred
By a whisper of love?
Spell-bound to a word
Does Time cease to move,
Till her calm grey eye
Expands to a sky
And the clouds of her hair
Like storms go by?

THE FALCON WOMAN

It is hard to be a man
Whose word is his bond
In love with such a woman,

When he builds on a promise
She lightly let fall
In carelessness of spirit.

The more sternly he asks her
To stand by that promise
The faster she flies.

But is it less hard
To be born such a woman
With wings like a falcon
And in carelessness of spirit
To love such a man?

TROUGHS OF SEA

'Do you delude yourself?' a neighbour asks,
Dismayed by my abstraction.
But though love cannot question love
Nor need deny its need,

Pity the man who finds a rebel heart
Under his breastbone drumming
Which reason warns him he should drown
In midnight wastes of sea.

Now as he stalks between tormented pines
(The moon in her last quarter)
A lissom spectre glides ahead
And utters not a word.

Waves tasselled with dark weed come rearing up
Like castle walls, disclosing
Deep in their troughs a ribbed sea-floor
To break his bones upon.

—Clasp both your hands under my naked foot
And press hard, as I taught you:
A trick to mitigate the pangs
Either of birth or love.

THE DEATH GRAPPLE

Lying between your sheets, I challenge
A watersnake in a swoln cataract
Or a starved lioness among drifts of snow.

Yet dare it out, for after each death grapple,
Each gorgon stare borrowed from very hate,
A childish innocent smile touches your lips,
Your eyelids droop, fearless and careless,
And sleep remoulds the lineaments of love.

THE STARRED COVERLET

A difficult achievement for true lovers
Is to lie mute, without embrace or kiss,
Without a rustle or a smothered sigh,
Basking each in the other's glory.

Let us not undervalue lips or arms
As reassurances of constancy,
Or speech as necessary communication
When troubled hearts go groping through the dusk;

Yet lovers who have learned this last refinement—
To lie apart, yet sleep and dream together
Motionless under their starred coverlet—
Crown love with wreaths of myrtle.

TURN OF THE MOON

Never forget who brings the rain
In swarthy goatskin bags from a far sea:
It is the Moon as she turns, repairing
Damages of long drought and sunstroke.

Never count upon rain, never foretell it,
For no power can bring rain
Except the Moon as she turns; and who can rule her?

She is prone to delay the necessary floods,
Lest such a gift might become obligation,
A month, or two, or three; then suddenly
Not relenting but by way of whim
Will perhaps conjure from the cloudless west
A single rain-drop to surprise with hope
Each haggard, upturned face.

Were the Moon a Sun, we would count upon her
To bring rain seasonably as she turned;
Yet no one thinks to thank the regular Sun
For shining fierce in summer, mild in winter—
Why should the Moon so drudge?

But if one night she brings us, as she turns,
Soft, steady, even, copious rain
That harms no leaf nor flower, but gently falls
Hour after hour, sinking to the tap roots,
And the sodden earth exhales at dawn
A long sigh scented with pure gratitude,
Such rain—the first rain of our lives, it seems,
Neither foretold, cajoled, nor counted on—
Is woman giving as she loves.

SELDOM YET NOW

Seldom yet now: the quality
Of this fierce love between us—
Seldom the encounter,
The presence always,
Free of oath or promise.

And if we were not so
But birds of similar plumage caged
In the peace of every day,
Would we still conjure wildfire up
From common earth, as now?

Song: A LOST WORLD

'Dear love, why should you weep
    For time's remorseless way?
Though today die in sleep
    And be called yesterday,
    We love, we stay.'

'I weep for days that died
    With former love that shone
On a world true and wide
    Before this newer one
    Which yours shines on.'

'Is this world not as true
    As that one ever was
Which now has fled from you
    Like shadows from the grass
    When the clouds pass?'

'Yet for that would I weep
    Kindly, before we kiss:
Love has a faith to keep
    With past felicities
    That weep for this.'

THE DANGEROUS GIFT

Were I to cut my hand
    On that sharp knife you gave me
    (That dangerous knife, your beauty),
I should know what to do:
    Bandage the wound myself
And hide the blood from you.

A murderous knife it is,
    As often you have warned me:
    For if I looked for pity
Or tried a wheedling note
    Either I must restore it
Or turn it on my throat.

TWICE OF THE SAME FEVER

No one can die twice of the same fever?
    Tell them it is untrue:
Have we not died three deaths, and three again,
    You of me, I of you?

The chill, the frantic pulse, brows burning,
    Lips broken by thirst—
Until, in darkness, a ghost grieves:
    'It was I died the first.'

Worse than such death, even, is resurrection.
    Do we dare laugh away
Disaster, and with a callous madrigal
    Salute the new day?

Part 5

RUBY AND AMETHYST

Two women: one as good as bread,
    Bound to a sturdy husband.
Two women: one as rare as myrrh,
    Bound only to herself.

Two women: one as good as bread,
    Faithful to every promise.
Two women: one as rare as myrrh,
    Who never pledges faith.

The one a flawless ruby wears
    But with such innocent pleasure
A stranger's eye might think it glass
    And take no closer look.

Two women: one as good as bread,
    The noblest of the city.
Two women: one as rare as myrrh,
    Who needs no public praise.

The pale rose-amethyst on her breast
    Has such a garden in it
Your eye could trespass there for hours,
    And wonder, and be lost.

About her head a swallow wheels
    Nor ever breaks the circuit:
Glory and awe of womanhood
    Still undeclared to man.

Two women: one as good as bread,
    Resistant to all weathers.
Two women: one as rare as myrrh,
    Her weather still her own.

RECOGNITION

When on the cliffs we met, by chance,
    I startled at your quiet voice
And watched the swallows round you dance
    Like children who had made a choice.

Simple it was, as I stood there,
    To penetrate the mask you wore,
Your secret lineage to declare
    And your lost dignities restore.

Yet thus I earned a poet's fee
    So far out-distancing desire
That swallows yell in rage at me
    As who would set their world on fire.

VARIABLES OF GREEN

Grass-green and aspen-green,
Laurel-green and sea-green,
Fine-emerald-green,
And many another hue:
As green commands the variables of green
So love my loves of you.

THE MEETING

We, two elementals, woman and man,
Approached each other from far away:
I on the lower wind, she on the upper.

And the faith with which we came invested
By the blind thousands of our twin worlds
Formed thunder clouds about us.

Never such uproar as when we met,
Nor such forked lightning; rain in a cataract
Tumbled on deserts dry these thousand years.

What of the meteorologists?
They said nothing, turned their faces away,
Let the event pass unrecorded.

And what of us? We also said nothing.
Is it not the height of silent humour
To cause an unknown change in the earth's climate?

NOT AT HOME

Her house loomed at the end of a Berkshire lane,
Tall but retired. She was expecting me,
And I approached with light heart and quick tread,
Having already seen from the garden gate
How bright her knocker shone—in readiness
For my confident rap?—and the steps holystoned.
I ran the last few paces, rapped and listened
Intently for the rustle of her approach. . . .

No reply, no movement. I waited three long minutes,
Then, in surprise, went down the path again
To observe the chimney stacks. No smoke from either.
And the curtains: were they drawn against the sun?
Or against what, then? I glanced over a wall
At her well-tended orchard, heavy with bloom
(Easter fell late that year, Spring had come early),
And found the gardener, bent over cold frames.

'Her ladyship is not at home?'
                                    'No, sir.'
'She was expecting me. My name is Lion.
Did she leave a note?'
                            'No, sir, she left no note.'
'I trust nothing has happened . . . ?'
                                    'No, sir, nothing. . . .
And yet she seemed preoccupied: we guess
Some family reason.'
                        '*Has* she a family?'
'That, sir, I could not say. . . . She seemed distressed—
Not quite herself, if I may venture so.'
'But she left no note?'
                        'Only a verbal message:
Her ladyship will be away some weeks
Or months, hopes to return before midsummer,
And, please, you are not to communicate.
There was something else: about the need for patience.'

The sun went in, a bleak wind shook the blossom,
Dust flew, the windows glared in a blank row. . . .
And yet I felt, when I turned slowly away,
Her eyes boring my back, as it might be posted
Behind a curtain slit, and still in love.

HORIZON

On a clear day how thin the horizon
Drawn between sea and sky,
Between sea-love and sky-love;
And after sunset how debatable
Even for an honest eye.

'Do as you will tonight,'
Said she, and so he did
By moonlight, candlelight,
Candlelight and moonlight,
While pillowed clouds the horizon hid.

Knowing-not-knowing that such deeds must end
In a curse which lovers long past weeping for
Had heaped upon him: she would be gone one night
With his familiar friend,
Granting him leave her beauty to explore
By moonlight, candlelight,
Candlelight and moonlight.

GOLDEN ANCHOR

Gone: and to an undisclosed region,
Free as the wind, if less predictable.
Why should I grieve, who have no claim on her?
My ring circles her finger, from her neck
Dangles my powerful jade. All is not lost
While still she wears those evident tokens
And no debts lie between us except love.

Or does the golden anchor plague her
As a drag on woman's liberty? Longing
To cut the cable, run grandly adrift,
Is she warned by a voice what wide misfortune
Ripples from ill faith?—therefore temporizes
And fears to use the axe, although consorting
With lovelessness and evil?

What should I say or do? It was she chose me,
Not contrariwise. Moreover, if I lavished
Extravagant praise on her, she deserved all.
I have been honest in love, as is my nature;
She secret, as is hers. I cannot grieve
Unless for having vexed her by unmasking
A jewelled virtue she was loth to use.

LION LOVER

You chose a lion to be your lover—
Me, who in joy such doom greeting
Dared jealously undertake
Cruel ordeals long foreseen and known,
Springing a trap baited with flesh: my own.

Nor would I now exchange this lion heart
For a less furious other,
Though by the Moon possessed
I gnaw at dry bones in a lost lair
And, when clouds cover her, roar my despair.

Gratitude and affection I disdain
As cheap in any market:
Your naked feet upon my scarred shoulders,
Your eyes naked with love,
Are all the gifts my beasthood can approve.

THE WINGED HEART

Trying to read the news, after your visit,
When the words made little sense, I let them go;
And found my heart suddenly sprouting feathers.

Alone in the house, and the full honest rain
After a devil's own four-day sirocco
Still driving down in sheets across the valley—

How it hissed, how the leaves of the olives shook!
We had suffered drought since earliest April;
Here we were already in October.

I have nothing more to tell you. What has been said
Can never possibly be retracted now
Without denial of the large universe.

Some curse had fallen between us, a dead hand,
An inhalation of evil sucking up virtue:
Which left us no recourse, unless we turned

Improvident as at our first encounter,
Deriding practical care of how or where:
Your certitude must be my certitude.

And the tranquil blaze of sky etherializing
The circle of rocks and our own rain-wet faces,
Was that not worth a lifetime of pure grief?

IN HER PRAISE

This they know well: the Goddess yet abides.
Though each new lovely woman whom she rides,
Straddling her neck a year or two or three,
Should sink beneath such weight of majesty
And, groping back to humankind, gainsay
The headlong power that whitened all her way
With a broad track of trefoil—leaving you,
Her chosen lover, ever again thrust through
With daggers, your purse rifled, your rings gone—
Nevertheless they call you to live on
To parley with the pure, oracular dead,
To hear the wild pack whimpering overhead,
To watch the Moon tugging at her cold tides.
Woman is mortal woman. She abides.

A RESTLESS GHOST

Alas for obstinate doubt: the dread
Of error in supposing my heart freed,
All care for her stone dead!
Ineffably will shine the hills and radiant coast
Of early morning when she is gone indeed,
Her divine elements disbanded, disembodied
And through the misty orchards in love spread—
When she is gone indeed—
But still among them moves her restless ghost.

BETWEEN MOON AND MOON

In the last sad watches of night
Hardly a sliver of light will remain
To edge the guilty shadow of a waned moon
That dawn must soon devour.
                            Thereafter, another
Crescent queen shall arise with power—
So wise a beauty never yet seen, say I:
A true creature of moon, though not the same
In nature, name or feature—
Her innocent eye rebuking inconstancy
As if Time itself should die and disappear.

So was it ever. She is here again, I sigh.

BEWARE, MADAM!

Beware, madam, of the witty devil,
The arch intriguer who walks disguised
In a poet's cloak, his gay tongue oozing evil.

Would you be a Muse? He will so declare you,
Pledging his blind allegiance,
Yet remain secret and uncommitted.

Poets are men: are single-hearted lovers
Who adore and trust beyond all reason,
Who die honourably at the gates of hell.

The Muse alone is licensed to do murder
And to betray: weeping with honest tears
She thrones each victim in her paradise.

But from this Muse the Devil borrows an art
That ill becomes a man. Beware, madam:
He plots to strip you bare of woman-pride.

He is capable of seducing your twin-sister
On the same pillow, and neither she nor you
Will suspect the act, so close a glamour he sheds.

Alas, being honourably single-hearted,
You adore and trust beyond all reason,
Being no more a Muse than he a poet.

ACROBATS

Poised impossibly on the high tight-rope
    Of love, in spite of all,
They still preserve their dizzying balance
And smile this way or that,
    As though uncertain on which side to fall.

OUZO UNCLOUDED

Here is ouzo (she said) to try you:
Better not drowned in water,
Better not chilled with ice,
Not sipped at thoughtfully,
Nor toped in secret.
Drink it down (she said) unclouded
At a blow, this tall glass full,
But keep your eyes on mine
Like a true Arcadian acorn-eater.

THE BROKEN GIRTH

Bravely from Fairyland he rode, on furlough,
Astride a tall bay given him by the Queen
From whose couch he had leaped not a half-hour since,
Whose lilies-of-the-valley shone from his helm.

But alas, as he paused to assist five Ulstermen
Sweating to raise a recumbent Ogham pillar,
Breach of a saddle-girth tumbled Oisín
To common Irish earth. At once, it is said,
Old age came on him with grief and frailty.

St Patrick asked: would he not confess the Christ?—
Which for that Lady's sake he loathed to do,
But northward loyally turned his eyes in death.
It was Fenians bore the unshriven corpse away
For burial, keening.
                    Curse me all squint-eyed monks
Who misconstrue the passing of Finn's son:
Old age, not Fairyland, was his delusion.

INKIDOO AND THE QUEEN OF BABEL

When I was a callant, born far hence,
You first laid hand on my innocence,
But sent your champion into a boar
That my fair young body a-pieces tore.

When I was a lapwing, crowned with gold,
Your lust and liking for me you told,
But plucked my feathers and broke my wing—
Wherefore all summer for grief I sing.

When I was a lion of tawny fell,
You stroked my mane and you combed it well,
But pitfalls seven you dug for me
That from one or other I might not flee.

When I was a courser, proud and strong,
That like the wind would wallop along,
You bated my pride with spur and bit
And many a rod on my shoulder split.

When I was a shepherd that for your sake
The bread of love at my hearth would bake,
A ravening wolf did you make of me
To be thrust from home by my brothers three.

When I tended your father's orchard close
I brought you plum, pear, apple, and rose,
But my lusty manhood away you stole
And changed me into a grovelling mole.

When I was simple, when I was fond,
Thrice and thrice did you wave your wand,
But now you vow to be leal and true
And softly ask, will I wed with you?

THREE SONGS FOR THE LUTE

I

TRUTH IS POOR PHYSIC

A wild beast falling sick
Will find his own best physic—
 Herb, berry, root of tree
Or wholesome salt to lick—
 And so run free.

But this I know at least
Better than a wild beast:
 That should I fall love-sick
And the wind veer to East,
 Truth is poor physic.

II

IN HER ONLY WAY

When her need for you dies
 And she wanders apart,
Never rhetoricize
 On the faithless heart,

But with manlier virtue
 Be content to say
She both loved you and hurt you
 In her only way.

III

HEDGES FREAKED WITH SNOW

No argument, no anger, no remorse,
  No dividing of blame.
There was poison in the cup—why should we ask
  From whose hand it came?

No grief for our dead love, no howling gales
  That through darkness blow,
But the smile of sorrow, a wan winter landscape,
  Hedges freaked with snow.

A TIME OF WAITING

The moment comes when my sound senses
Warn me to keep the pot at a quiet simmer,
Conclude no rash decisions, enter into
No random friendships, check the runaway tongue
And fix my mind in a close caul of doubt—
Which is more difficult, maybe, than to face
Night-long assaults of lurking furies.

The pool lies almost empty; I watch it nursed
By a thin stream. Such idle intervals
Are from waning moon to the new—a moon always
Holds the cords of my heart. Then patience, hands!
Dabble your nerveless fingers in the shallows;
A time shall come when she has need of them.

EXPECT NOTHING

Give, ask for nothing, hope for nothing,
Subsist on crumbs, though scattered casually
Not for you (she smiles) but for the birds.
Though only a thief's diet, it staves off
Dire starvation, nor does she grow fat
On the bread she crumbles, while the lonely truth
Of love is honoured, and her word pledged.

NO LETTER

Be angry with yourself, as well you may,
But why with her? She is no party to
Those avaricious dreams that pester you.
Why knot your fists as though plotting to slay
Even our postman George (whose only due
Is a small Christmas box on Christmas Day)
If his delivery does not raise the curse
Of doubt from your impoverished universe?

THE WHY OF THE WEATHER

Since no one knows the why of the weather
Or can authoritatively forecast
More than twelve hours of day or night, at most,
Every poor fool is licenced to explain it
As Heaven's considered judgement on mankind—
And I to account for its vagaries, Myrto,
By inklings of your unaccountable mind.

IN TIME

In time all undertakings are made good,
All cruelties remedied,
Each bond resealed more firmly than before—
Befriend us, Time, Love's gaunt executor!

JUGUM IMPROBUM

Pyrrha, jugo tandem vitulum junges-ne leoni?
Sit tibi dilectus, num stricto verbere debet
Compelli pavitans medium moriturus in ignem?

AT BEST, POETS

Woman with her forests, moons, flowers, waters,
And watchful fingers:
We claim no magic comparable to hers—
At best, poets; at worst, sorcerers.

SHE IS NO LIAR

She is no liar, yet she will wash away
Honey from her lips, blood from her shadowy hand,
And, dressed at dawn in clean white robes will say,
Trusting the ignorant world to understand:
'Such things no longer are; this is today.'

THE LEAP

Forget the rest: my heart is true
And in its waking thought of you
Gives the same wild and sudden leap
That jerks it from the brink of sleep.

JUDGEMENT OF PARIS

What if Prince Paris, after taking thought,
Had not adjudged the apple to Aphrodite
But, instead, had favoured buxom Hera,
Divine defendress of the marriage couch?
What if Queen Helen had been left to squander
Her beauty upon the thralls of Menelaus,
Hector to die unhonoured in his bed,
Penthesileia to hunt a poorer quarry,
The bards to celebrate a meaner siege?
Could we still have found the courage, you and I,
To embark together for Cranaë
And consummate our no less fateful love?

MAN DOES, WOMAN IS

Studiously by lamp-light I appraised
The palm of your hand, its heart-line
Identical with its head-line;
And you appraised the wondering frown.

I spread my cards face-upwards on the table,
Not challenging you for yours.
Man does; but woman is—
Can a gamester argue with his luck?

THE THREE-FACED

Who calls her two-faced? Faces, she has three:
The first inscrutable, for the outer world;
The second shrouded in self-contemplation;
The third, her face of love,
Once for an endless moment turned on me.

DAZZLE OF DARKNESS

The flame guttered, flared impossibly high,
Went out for good; yet in the dazzle of darkness
I saw her face ashine like an angel's:
Beauty too memorable for lamentation,
Though doomed to rat and maggot.

MYRRHINA

O, why judge Myrrhina
As though she were a man?
She obeys a dark wisdom
(As Eve did before her)
Which never can fail,
Being bound by no pride
Of armorial bearings
Bequeathed in tail male.

And though your blood brother
Who dared to do you wrong
In his greed for Myrrhina
Might plead a like wisdom
The fault to excuse,
Myrrhina is just:
She has hanged the poor rogue
By the neck from her noose.

FOOD OF THE DEAD

Blush as you stroke the curves—chin, lips and brow—
Of your scarred face, Prince Orpheus: for she has called it
Beautiful, nor would she stoop to flattery.
Yet are you patient still, when again she has eaten
Food of the dead, seven red pomegranate-seeds,
And once more warmed the serpent at her thighs
For a new progress through new wards of hell?

I WILL WRITE

He had done for her all that a man could,
And, some might say, more than a man should,
Then was ever a flame so recklessly blown out
Or a last goodbye so negligent as this?
'I will write to you,' she muttered briefly,
Tilting her cheek for a polite kiss;
Then walked away, nor ever turned about. . . .

Long letters written and mailed in her own head—
There are no mails in a city of the dead.

Part 6

BIRD OF PARADISE

At sunset, only to his true love,
The bird of paradise opened wide his wings
Displaying emerald plumage shot with gold
Unguessed even by him.
                    True, that wide crest
Had blazoned royal estate, and the tropic flowers
Through which he flew had shown example
Of what brave colours gallantry might flaunt,
But these were other. She asked herself, trembling:
'What did I do to awake such glory?'

THE METAPHOR

The act of love seemed a dead metaphor
For love itself, until the timeless moment
When fingers trembled, heads clouded,
And love rode everywhere, too numinous
To be expressed or greeted calmly:
O, then it was, deep in our own forest,
We dared revivify the metaphor,
Shedding the garments of this epoch
In scorn of time's wilful irrelevancy;
So at last understood true nakedness
And the long debt to silence owed.

SECRECY

Lovers are happy
When favoured by chance,
But here is blessedness
Beyond all happiness,

Not to be gainsaid
By any gust of chance,
Harvest of one vine,
Gold from the same mine:

To keep which sacred
Demands a secrecy
That the world might blame
As deceit and shame;

Yet to publish which
Would make a him and her
Out of me and you
That were both untrue.

Let pigeons couple
Brazenly on the bough,
But royal stag and hind
Are of our own mind.

JOSEPH AND MARY

They turned together with a shocked surprise—
He, old and fabulous; she, young and wise—
Both having heard a newborn hero weep
In convalescence from the stroke of sleep.

THE OLEASTER

Each night for seven nights beyond the gulf
A storm raged, out of hearing, and crooked flashes
Of lightning animated us. Before day-break
Rain fell munificently for the earth's need. . . .

No, here they never plant the sweet olive
As some do (bedding slips in a prepared trench),
But graft it on the club of Hercules
The savage, inexpugnable oleaster
Whose roots and bole bunching from limestone crannies
Sprout impudent shoots born only to be lopped
Spring after Spring. Theirs is a loveless berry. . . .

By mid-day we walk out, with naked feet,
Through pools on the road, gazing at waterfalls
Or a line of surf, but mostly at the trees
Whose elegant branches rain has duly blackened
And pressed their crowns to a sparkling silver.

Innumerable, plump with promise of oil,
The olives hang grass-green, in thankfulness
For a bitter sap and bitter New Year snows
That cleansed their bark. . . .
                                        Forgive me, dearest love,
If nothing I can say be strange or new.
I am no child of the hot South like you,
Though in rock rooted like an oleaster.

NON COGUNT ASTRA

Come, live in Now and occupy it well.
Prediction's no alternative to forethought
Despite at least four hundred arts of scrying
The dubious future, such as to study birds,
Or bull's guts, or sheep droppings, or wine lees
In an alabaster cup. True, the most ancient
Most exact discipline, astrology,
Comes hallowed by a college of gowned mantics
Who still cast horoscopes only by stars
Apparent to the still unaided eye—
And of whom a few, the best, focus their powers
On exact horary configurations, then
At an agreed moment brusquely sweep away
Zodiacal signs, conjunctions, trines,
And reinduce a pure, archaic vision;
Yet disregard all false astrologers
Who dare lay greedy or compulsive hands
On the stars you sped at your nativity
Along their courses and forbad to canker
The rose of love or blunt the blade of honour:
No public hangmen these, but servants chosen
To wear bright livery at your house gate;
And favour you the more, the less you fear them.

Song: SWORD AND ROSE

The King of Hearts a broadsword bears,
  The Queen of Hearts, a rose—
Though why, not every gambler cares
  Or cartomancer knows.

Be beauty yours, be honour mine,
  Yet sword and rose are one:
Great emblems that in love combine
  Until the dealing's done;

For no card, whether small or face,
  Shall overtrump our two
Except that Heart of Hearts, the Ace,
  To which their title's due.

ENDLESS PAVEMENT

In passage along an endless, eventless pavement,
None but the man in love, as he turns to stare
At the glazed eyes flickering past, will remain aware
Of his own, assured, meticulous, rustic tread—
As if pavement were pebbles, or rocks overgrown by grasses;
And houses, trees with birds flying overhead.

IN DISGUISE

Almost I welcome the dirty subterfuges
Of this unreal world closing us in,
That present you as a lady of high fashion
And me as a veteran on the pensioned list.

Our conversation is infinitely proper,
With a peck on either cheek as we meet or part—
Yet the seven archons of the heavenly stair
Tremble at the disclosure of our seals.

A MEASURE OF CASUALNESS

Too fierce the candlelight; your gentle voice
Roars as in dream; my shoulder-nooks flower;
A scent of honeysuckle invades the house,
And my fingertips are so love-enhanced
That sailcloth feels like satin to them.
Teach me a measure of casualness
Though you stalk into my room like Venus naked.

IN TIME OF ABSENCE

Lovers in time of absence need not signal
With call and answering call:
By sleight of providence each sends the other
A clear, more than coincidental answer
To every still unformulated puzzle,
Or a smile at a joke harboured, not yet made,
Or power to be already wise and unafraid.

THE GREEN CASTLE

The first heaven is a flowery plain;
The second, a glass mountain;
The third, likewise terrestrial,
Is an orchard-close unclouded
By prescience of death or change
Or the blood-sports of desire:
Our childhood paradise.

The next three heavens, known as celestial,
Are awkward of approach.
Mind is the prudent rider; body, the ass
Disciplined always by a harsh bit,
Accepts his daily diet of thorns
And frugal, brackish water;
Holds converse with archangels.

The seventh heaven, most unlike those others,
We once contrived to enter
By a trance of love; it is a green castle
Girdled with ramparts of blue sea
And silent but for the waves' leisured wash.
There Adam rediscovered Eve:
She wrapped him in her arms.

An afterglow of truth, still evident
When we had fallen earthward,
Astonished all except the born blind.
Strangers would halt us in the roadway:
'Confess where you have been.'
And, at a loss, we replied stumblingly:
'It was here, it was nowhere—
Last night we lodged at a green castle,
Its courtyard paved with gold.'

NOT TO SLEEP

Not to sleep all the night long, for pure joy,
Counting no sheep and careless of chimes,
Welcoming the dawn confabulation
Of birds, her children, who discuss idly
Fanciful details of the promised coming—
Will she be wearing red, or russet, or blue,
Or pure white?—whatever she wears, glorious:
Not to sleep all the night long, for pure joy,
This is given to few but at last to me,
So that when I laugh and stretch and leap from bed
I shall glide downstairs, my feet brushing the carpet
In courtesy to civilized progression,
Though, did I wish, I could soar through the open window
And perch on a branch above, acceptable ally
Of the birds still alert, grumbling gently together.

THE HEARTH

Here it begins: the worm of love breeding
Among red embers of a hearth-fire
Turns to a chick, is slowly fledged,
And will hop from lap to lap in a ring
Of eager children basking at the blaze.

But the luckless man who never sat there,
Nor borrowed live coals from the sacred source
To warm a hearth of his own making,
Nor bedded lay under pearl-grey wings
In dutiful content,

How shall he watch at the stroke of midnight
Dove become phoenix, plumed with green and gold?
Or be caught up by jewelled talons
And haled away to a fastness of the hills
Where an unveiled woman, black as Mother Night,
Teaches him a new degree of love
And the tongues and songs of birds?

THE BEDS OF GRAINNE AND DIARMUID

How many secret nooks in copse or glen
We sained for ever with our pure embraces,
No man shall know; though indeed master-poets
Reckon one such for every eve of the year,
To sain their calendar.
                            But this much is true:
That children stumbling on our lairs by chance
In quest of hazel-nuts or whortleberries
Will recognize the impress of twin bodies
On the blue-green turf, starred with diversity
Of alien flowers, and shout astonishment.
Yet should some amorous country pair, presuming
To bask in joy on any bed of ours,
Offend against the love by us exampled,
Long ivy roots will writhe up from beneath
And bitterly fetter ankle, wrist and throat.

THE BLACK GODDESS

Silence, words into foolishness fading,
Silence prolonged, of thought so secret
We hush the sheep-bells and the loud cicada.

And your black agate eyes, wide open, mirror
The released firebird beating his way
Down a whirled avenue of blues and yellows.

Should I not weep? Profuse the berries of love,
The speckled fish, the filberts and white ivy
Which you, with a half-smile, bestow
On your delectable broad land of promise
For me, who never before went gay in plumes.

BETWEEN TRAINS

Arguing over coffee at the station,
Neither of us noticed her dark beauty,
Though she sat close by, until suddenly
Three casual words—does it matter what they were?—
Spoken without remarkable intonation
Or accent, so bewildered you and me,
As it were catching the breath of our conversation,
That each set down his coffee-cup, to stare.
'You have come for us?' my lips cautiously framed—
Her eyes were almost brighter than I could bear—
But she rose and left, unready to be named.

TO THE TEUMESSIAN VIXEN

Do not mistake me: I was never a rival
  Of that poor fox who pledged himself to win
Your heart by gnawing away his brush. Who ever
  Proved love was love except by a whole skin?

THE HUNG WU VASE

With women like Marie no holds are barred.
Where do they get the gall? How can they do it?

She stormed out, slamming the hall door so hard
That a vase on the gilt shelf above—you knew it,
Loot from the Summer Palace at Pekin
And worth the entire contents of my flat—
Toppled and fell. . . .
                  I poured myself straight gin,
Downing it at a gulp. 'So that was that!'

The bell once more. . . . Marie walked calmly in,
Observed broken red porcelain on the mat,
Looked up, looked down again with condescension,
Then, gliding past me to retrieve a glove
(Her poor excuse for this improper call),
Muttered: 'And one thing I forget to mention:
Your Hung Wu vase was phoney, like your love!'

How can they do it? Where do they get the gall?

LA MEJICANA

Perfect beneath an eight-rayed sun you lie,
   Rejoiced at his caresses. Yours is a land
For pumas, chillis, and men dark of eye;
   Yet summon me with no derisive hand
From these remote moon-pastures drenched in dew—
And watch who burns the blacker: I or you.

LAMIA IN LOVE (revision)

Need of this man was her ignoble secret:
Desperate for love, yet loathing to deserve it,
She wept pure tears of sorrow when his eyes
Betrayed mistrust of her impeccable lies.

Song: ALL I TELL YOU FROM MY HEART

I begged my love to wait a bit
    Although the sky was clear:
'I smell a shower of rain,' said I,
    'And you'll be caught, I fear.'
'You want to keep me trapped,' she said,
    'And hold my hand again. . . .'
But not ten minutes had she gone
    When how the rain did rain!

'Alas, dear love, so wet you are—
    You should have trusted me!
For all I tell you from my heart
    Is sure as prophecy.'

I begged my love to wait a bit
    And watch the faggots blaze.
'There's a music on the march,' said I,
    'To cheer whoever stays.'
'You want to keep me trapped,' she said,
    'O, every night's the same. . . .'
But not ten minutes had she gone
    When in the fiddlers came!

'Alas, dear love, what tunes they played—
    You should have trusted me!
For all I tell you from my heart
    Is sure as prophecy.'

I begged my love to take good heed
    When walking through the wood,
And warned her of a random rogue
    Who brought the world no good.
'You want to keep me trapped,' she said,
    'And roll me in your bed. . . .'
But scarce a hundred yards from home
    She lost her maidenhead.

'Alas, dear love, it is too late—
    You should have trusted me!
For all I told you from my heart
    Was sure as prophecy.'

THE UNDEAD

To be the only woman alive in a vast hive of death
Is a strange predicament, granted! Innumerable zombies
With glazed eyes shuffle around at their diurnal tasks,
Keep the machines whirring, drudge idly in stores and bars,
Bear still-born zombie children, pack them off to school
For education in science and the dead languages,
Divert themselves with moribund travesties of living,
Lay mountainous bets on horses never seen to run,
Speed along highways in conveyor-belt automobiles
But, significantly enough, often dare overshoot
The traffic signals and *boing!* destroy themselves again,
Earning expensive funerals. (These, if at last they emerge
From the select green cemetery plots awarded them
On their twenty-first death-days by sombre uncles and aunts,
Will become zombies of the second degree, reverenced
Nationwide in church or synagogue.)
                                        Nevertheless,
Let none of this daunt you, child! Accept it as your fate
To live, to love, knowingly to cause true miracles,
Nor ever to find your body possessed by a cold corpse.
For one day, as you choose an unfamiliar side-street
Keeping both eyes open, alert, not apprehensive,
You shall suddenly (this is a promise) come to a brief halt:
For striding towards you on the same pavement will appear
A young man with the halo of life around his head,
Will catch you reassuringly by both hands, asseverating
In phrases utterly unintelligible to a zombie
That all is well: you are neither diseased, deranged, nor mistaken—
But merely undead. He will name others like you, no less alive:
Two girls and a man, all moneyless immigrants arrived
Lately at a new necropolitan conurbation.
'*Come with me, girl, and join them! The dead, you will observe,*
Can exercise no direct sanctions against the living
And therefore doggedly try to omit them from all the records.
Still, they cannot avoid a certain morbid fascination
With what they call our genius. They will venture questions
But never wait for an answer—being doubtless afraid
That it will make their ears burn, or their eyes prick with tears—
Nor can they countermand what orders we may issue.'

Nod your assent, go with him, do not even return to pack!
When five live people room together, each rates as a million—
But encourage the zombies to serve you, the honest creatures,
For though one cannot ameliorate their way of death
By telling them true stories or singing them real songs,
They will feel obscurely honoured by your warm presence.

GRACE NOTES

It was not the words, nor the melody,
  Not the beat, nor the pace;
It was that slow suspension of our breathing
  As we watched your face,
And the grace-notes, unrecordable on the clef,
  Sung only by a spirit in grace.

Part 7

ABOVE THE EDGE OF DOOM

Bats at play taunt us with 'guess how many'!
And music sounds far off, tempered by sea.
Above the edge of doom sits woman
Communing with herself. 'Dear Love', says she,
As it were apostrophizing cat or dog,
'Sometimes by a delicate glance and gesture
You almost seem to understand me,
Poor honest creature of the blue eyes,
Having crept closer to my sealed bosom
With your more desperate faith in womankind
Than any other since I first flowered.

It may be best you cannot read my mind'.

WILD CYCLAMEN

'What can I do for you'? she asked gently.
I reached for pen and paper: 'Draw me flowers!'

She pursed her lips—o, the smooth brown forehead,
The smooth lips drooped, intent on their task!—
And drew me wild Majorcan cyclamen
(Not yet in season) extravagantly petalled,
Then laughed and tossed me back the picture.

'It is nothing', she said; yet that cyclamen odour
Hung heavy in the room for a long while;
And when she was gone, I caught myself smiling
In her own crooked way, trying to make my eyes
Sparkle like hers, though ineffectually,
Till I fell asleep; for this was my sick-bed
And her visits brief, by order.

BATXOCA

Firm-lipped, high-breasted, slender Queen of Bean-stalk land,
Who are more to me than any woman upon this earth
Though you live from hand to mouth, keeping no certain hours,
Disguising your wisdom with unpracticality
And your elusiveness with hugs for all and sundry,
Flaunting green, yellow and scarlet, suddenly disappearing
In a whirlwind rage and flurry of skirts, always alone
Until found, days later, asleep on a couch of broom
And incommunicable until you have breakfasted—
By what outrageous freak of dissimilarity
Were you forced, noble Batxóca, to fall so deep in love
With me as to demand marriage, despite your warning
That you and I must on no account be seen together—
A Beanstalk Queen, no less, paired with a regular man!—
Did you wistfully, perhaps, expect me to say 'no'?

THE SNAP-COMB WILDERNESS

Magic is tangled in a woman's hair
For the enlightenment of male pride.
To slide a comb uxoriously
Through an even swell of tresses undisturbed
By their cascade from an exact parting
Could never hearten or enlighten me—
Not though her eyes were bluer than blue sea.
Magic rules an irreducible jungle
Dark as eclipse and scented with despair,
A stubborn snap-comb wilderness of hair,
Each strand a singular, wild, curling tree.

CHANGE

'This year she has changed greatly,'—meaning you—
My sanguine friends agree,
And hope thereby to reassure me.

No, child, you never change; neither do I—
Indeed all our lives long
We are still fated to do wrong,

Too fast caught by care of humankind
Easily vexed and grieved,
Foolishly flattered and deceived;

And yet each knows that the changeless other
Must love and pardon still,
Be the new error what it will:

Assured by that same glint of deathlessness
Which neither can surprise
In any other pair of eyes.

A COURT OF LOVE

Were you to break the vow we swore together,
The vow, I said, would break you utterly:
Despite your pleas of duty elsewhere owed,
You could no longer laugh, work, heal, do magic,
Nor in the mirror face your own eyes.

They have summoned me before their Court of Love
And warned me I must sign for your release
Pledging my word never again to draft
A similar pact, as one who has presumed
Lasting felicity still unknown in time.
What should I do? Forswear myself for you?
No man in love, plagued by his own scruples,
Will ever, voluntarily, concede
That women have a spirit above vows.

BLACK

Black drinks the sun and draws all colours to it.
I am bleached white, my truant love. Come back
And stain me with intensity of black.

BETWEEN HYSSOP AND AXE

To know our destiny is to know the horror
Of separation, dawn oppressed by night:
Is, between hyssop and axe, boldly to prove
That gifted, each, with singular need for freedom
And haunted, both, by spectres of reproach,
We may yet house together without succumbing
To the low fever of domesticity
Or to the lunatic spin of aimless flight.

GOLD AND MALACHITE

After the hour of illumination, when the tottering mind
Has been by force delivered from its incubus of despair,
When all the painted papier-mâché Mexican faces
Of demons grinning at you from Hell's vaulted roof
Fade and become angelic monitors of wisdom—
Slowly the brisk intelligence wakes, to mutter questions
Of when, where, how, which should be the first step forward . . .

Now is the crucial moment you were forewarned against.
Stop your ears with your fingers, guard unequivocal silence
Lest you discuss wisdom in the language of unwisdom.
Roam instead through the heaped treasury of your heart:
You will find her, from whom you have been so long estranged,
Chin to knees, brooding apart on gold and malachite.
But beware again: even a shy embrace would be too explicit—
Let her learn by your gait alone that you are free at last.

AMBIENCE

The nymph of the forest, only in whose honour
These birds perform, provides an ambience
But never leads the chorus: even at dawn
When we awake to whistle, flute and pipe,
Astonished they can so extemporize
Their own parts, as it were haphazard
Each in his own time, yet avoid discordance
Or domineering, however virtuose
Or long-sustained each voluntary of love.
The rare silences, too, appear like sound
Rather than pause for breath or meditation . . .
Nor is the same piece ever given twice.

THE VOW

The vow once sworn may never be annulled
Except by a higher law of love or mercy—
Search your heart well: is there a lie hidden
Deep in its convolutions of resolve?

For whom do you live? Can it be for yourself?
For whom then? Not for this unlovely world,
Not for the rotting waters of mischance,
Nor for the tall eventual catafalque.

You live for her who alone loves you,
Whose royal prerogative can be denied
By none observant of the awakening gasps
That greet her progress down whatever hall.

Your vow is to truth, not practicality;
To honour, not to the dead world's esteem;
To a bed of rock, not to a swan's-down pillow;
To the tears you kiss away from her black eyes.

They lament an indestructible world of men
Who dare not listen or watch, but challenge proof
That a leap of a thousand miles is nothing
And to walk invisibly needs no artifice.

THE FROG AND THE GOLDEN BALL

She let her golden ball fall down the well
   And begged a cold frog to retrieve it;
For which she kissed his ugly, gaping mouth—
   Indeed, he could scarce believe it.

And seeing him transformed to his princely shape,
   Who had been by hags enchanted,
She knew she could never love another man
   Nor by any fate be daunted.

But what would her royal father and mother say?
   They had promised her in marriage
To a cousin whose wide kingdom marched with theirs,
   Who rode in a jewelled carriage.

'Our plight, dear heart, would appear past human hope
   To all but you and me: in fact to all
Who have never swum as a frog in a dark well
   Or have lost a golden ball.'

'What then shall we do now?' she asked her lover.
   He kissed her again and said:
'Is magic of love less powerful at your Court
   Than at this green well-head?'

THOSE WHO CAME SHORT

Those who came short of love for me or you,
Where are they now? Ill-starred and bitter-mouthed,
Cursing us for their own contrariness,
Each having fallen in turn, head over heels,
From that illusive heaven at which they flew.

Are we then poison of love-perfection
To all but our own kind? Should we beware
Of handling such intemperate shaggy creatures
As leap on us like dogs to be cosseted
And, after, claim full rights of jealousy?

At once too simple and too various
Except for ourselves, should we awhile conceal
Our studies from the world, in cool forbearance
Watching each night for another dawn to break
And the last guest to straggle home?

WHOSE LOVE

Every choice is always the wrong choice,
Every vote cast is always cast away—
How can truth hover between alternatives?

Then love me more than dearly, love me wholly,
Love me with no weighing of circumstance
As I am pledged in honour to love you:
With no weakness, with no speculation
On what might happen should you and I prove less
Than bringers-to-be of our own certainty.
Neither was born by hazard: each foreknew
The extreme possession we are grown into.

THIS HOLY MOUTH

The demon who throughout our late estrangement
Followed with malice in my footsteps, often
Making as if to stumble, so that I stumbled
And gashed my head against a live rook;
Who tore my palms on butcher's broom and thorn
Flung me at midnight into filthy ditches
And multiplied the horrors of this house
When back I limped again to a hard bed;
Who simultaneously plagued you too
With sleeplessness, dismay and darkness,
Paralysed your hands, denied you air—
We both know well he was the same demon
Arch-enemy of rule and calculation,
Who lives for our love, being created from it,
Astonishes us with blossom, silvers the hills
With more than moonlight, summons bees in swarms
From the Lion's mouth to fill our lives with honey,
Turns flesh into fire, and eyes into deep lakes
And so may do once more, this holy mouth.

THE BLOW

You struck me on the face and I, who strike
Only to kill, stood in confusion like
Death's fool: your ugly blow
Had fallen soft as snow.

Love me for what I am, with liberty
To curb my rage; I love you for what will be—
Your urgent sun—therefore
Acquitting you of error.

Laughter becomes us: gift of the third eye
That passes nothing by.

THE IMPOSSIBLE

Dear love, since the impossible proves
    Our sole recourse from this distress,
Claim it: the ebony ritual-mask of no
    Cannot outstare a living yes.

Claim it without despond or hate
    Or greed; but in your gentler tone
Say: 'This is ours, the impossible,' and silence
    Will give consent it is ours alone,

The impossible has wild-cat claws
    Which you would rather meet and die
Than commit love to time's curative venom
    And break our oath; for so would I.

THE FETTER

Concerned, against our wish, with a sick world,
Self-neglectful, deaf to knock or summons,
We make amends for follies not our own.

We have taken love through a thousand deaths:
Should either try to slip our iron fetter,
It bites yet deeper into neck and arm.

As for that act of supererogation,
The kiss in which we secretly concur,
Let laughter mitigate its quiet excess.

Could we only be a simple, bickering pair
In the tied cottage of a small estate
With no tasks laid on us except to dig,

Hoe, fatten geese and scrape the quarter's rent,
How admirable our close interdependence;
Our insecurity, how fortunate!

IRON PALACE

We stood together, side by side, rooted
In the iron heart of circumambient hills,
Parents to a new age, weeping in awe
That the lot had fallen, of all mankind, on us
Now sealed as love's exemplars.

We could not prevaricate or argue,
Citing involvement in some alien scene,
Nor plead unworthiness; none else could venture
To live detached from force of circumstance
As history neared its ending.

We told no one. These were not strange dreams
Recalled at breakfast with a yawning smile,
Nor tales for children, on the verge of sleep,
Who ask no questions. Our predicament
Remained a silent burden.

We had no token or proof and needed none
Of what we learned that day; but laughed softly,
Watching our hands engage, in co-awareness
That these red hills warned us, on pain of death,
Never to disengage them.

Woman, wild and hard as the truth may be,
Nothing can circumvent it. We stand coupled
With chains, who otherwise might live apart
Conveniently paired, each with another,
And slide securely graveward.

TRUE JOY

Whoever has drowned and awhile entered
The adamantine gates of afterwards,
Stands privileged to reject heavenly joy
(Though without disrespect for God's archangels)
With 'never again'—no moon, no herbs, no sea,
No singular love of women.

True joy, believe us, is to groan and wake
From the crowded merry-make on Fiddler's Green,
With lungs now emptied of salt water,
With gradual heat returning to clammed veins
In the first flicker of reanimation,
Repossession of now, awareness
Of her live hands and lips, her playful voice,
Her smooth and wingless shoulders.

THE HIDDEN GARDEN

Nor can ambition make this garden theirs,
Any more than birds can fly through a windowpane.
When they hint at passwords, keys and private stairs,
We are tempted often to open the front gate
Which has no lock, and haul them bodily in,
Abashed that there they wait, disconsolate.

And yet such pity would be worse than pride:
Should we approve as love their vain self-pity,
The gate must vanish and we be left outside.

SON ALTESSE

Alone, you are no more than many another
Gay-hearted, greedy, passionate noblewoman;
And I, alone, no more than a slow-witted
Passionate, credulous knight, though skilled in fight.

Then if I hail you as my Blessed Virgin
This is no flattery, nor does it endow you
With private magic which, when I am gone,
May flatter rogues or drunken renegades.

Name me your single, proud, wholehearted champion
Whose feats no man alive will overpass;
But they must reverence you as I do: only
Conjoined in fame will we grow legendary.

Should I ride home, vainglorious after battle,
With droves of prisoners and huge heaps of spoil,
Make me dismount a half mile from your door:
To walk barefoot in dust, as a knight must.

Yet never greet me carelessly or idly,
Nor use the teasing manners learned at Court,
Lest I be ambushed in a treacherous pass—
And you pent up in shame's black nunnery.

EVERYWHERE IS HERE

By this exchange of eyes, this encirclement
You of me, I of you, together we baffle
Logic no doubt, but never understanding;
And laugh instead of choking back the tears
When we say good-bye.
                     Fog gathers thick about us
Yet a single careless pair of leaves, one green, one gold,
Whirl round and round each other skippingly
As though blown by a wind; pause and subside
In a double star, the gold above the green.

Everywhere is here, once we have shattered
The iron-bound laws of contiguity,
Blazoning love as an eagle with four wings
(Their complementary tinctures counterchanged)
That scorns to roost on any temple tower.

Song: THE FAR SIDE OF YOUR MOON

The far side of your moon is black,
   And glorious grows the vine;
Ask anything of me you lack,
   But only what is mine.

Yours is the great wheel of the Sun,
   And yours the unclouded sky;
Then take my stars, take every one
   But wear them openly,

Walking in splendour through the plain
   For all the world to see,
Since none alive shall view again
   The match of you and me.

DELIVERANCE

Lying disembodied under the trees
(Their slender trunks converged above us
Like rays of a fivefold star) we heard
A sudden whinnying from the dark hill.

Our implacable demon, foaled by love,
Never knew rein or saddle; though he drank
From a stream winding by, his blue pastures
Ranged far out beyond the stellar mill.

He had seared us two so close together
That death itself might not disjoin us;
It was impossible you could love me less,
It was impossible I could love you more.

We were no calculating lovers
But gasped in awe at our deliverance
From a too familiar prison,
And vainly puzzled how it was that now
We should never need to build another,
As each, time after time, had done before.

CONJUNCTION

What happens afterwards, none need enquire:
They are poised there in conjunction, beyond time,
At an oak-tree top level with Paradise:
Its leafy tester unshaken where they stand
Palm to palm, mouth to mouth, beyond desire,
Perpetuating lark song, perfume, colour,
And the tremulous gasp of watchful winds,

Past all unbelief, we know them held
By peace and light and irrefragable love
Twin paragons, our final selves, resistant
To the dull pull of earth dappled with shade:
Myself, the forester, never known to abandon
His vigilant coursing of the forest floor,
And you, dryad of dryads, never before
Yielding her whole heart to the enemy, man.

NOTHING NOW ASTONISHES

A month of vigilance draws to its close
With silence of snow and the Northern Lights
In longed-for wordlessness.

This rainbow spanning our two worlds
Becomes more than a bridge between them:
They fade into geography.

Variegated with the seven colours,
We twist them into skeins for hide and seek
In a lovers' labyrinth.

Can I be astonished at male trembling
Of sea-horizons as you lean towards them?
Nothing now astonishes.

You change, from a running drop of pure gold
On a silver salver, to the white doe
In nut-groves harbouring.

Let me be changed now to an eight-petalled
Scarlet anemone that will never strain
For the circling butterfly.

Rest, my loud heart: your too exultant flight
Had raised the wing-beat to a roar
Drowning seraphic whispers.

POSTSCRIPT

I'd die for you, or you for me,
So furious is our jealousy—
And if you doubt this to be true
Kill me outright, lest I kill you.

Part 8

COCK IN PULLET'S FEATHERS

Though ready enough with beak and spurs,
You go disguised, a cock in pullet's feathers,
Among those crowing, preening chanticleers.
But, dear self, learn to love your own body
In its full naked glory,
Despite all blemishes of moles and scars—

As she, for whom it shines, wholly loves hers.

ARREARS OF MOONLIGHT

My heart lies wrapped in red under your pillow,
My body wanders banished among the stars;
On one terrestial pretext or another
You still withhold the extravagant arrears
Of moonlight that you owe me,
Though the owl whoops from a far olive branch
His brief, monotonous, night-long reminder.

WHAT DID YOU SAY?

She listened to his voice urgently pleading,
So captivated by his eloquence
She saw each word in its own grace and beauty
Drift like a flower down that clear-flowing brook,
And draw a wake of multicoloured bubbles.
But when he paused, intent on her reply,
She could stammer only: 'Love, what did you say'?—
As loath as ever to hold him in her arms
Naked, under the trees, until high day.

LURE OF MURDER

A round moon suffocates the neighbouring stars
With greener light than sun through vine-leaves.
Awed by her ecstasy of solitude
I crouch among rocks, scanning the gulf, agape,
Whetting a knife on my horny sole.

Alas for the lure of murder, dear my love!
Could its employment purge two moon-vexed hearts
Of jealousy more formidable than death,
Then each would stab, stab, stab at secret parts
Of the other's beloved body where unknown
Zones of desire imperil full possession.

But never can mortal dagger serve to geld
This glory of ours, this loving beyond reason—
Death holds no remedy or alternative:
We are singled out to endure his lasting grudge
On the tall battlements of nightfall.

THE GORGE

Yonder beyond all hopes of access
Begins your queendom; here is my frontier.
Between us howl phantoms of the long dead,
But the bridge that I cross, concealed from view
Even in sunlight, and the gorge bottomless,
Swings and echoes under a strong tread
Because of my need for you.

ECSTASY OF CHAOS

When the immense drugged universe explodes
In a cascade of unendurable colour
And leaves us gasping naked,
This is no more than ecstasy of chaos:
Hold fast, with both hands, to the royal love
Which alone, as we know certainly, restores
Fragmentation into true being.

STOLEN JEWEL

You weep wholeheartedly—your shining tears
Roll down for sorrow, not like mine for joy.
Dear love, should we not scorn to treat each other
With palliatives and with placebos?

Under a blinding moon you took from me
This jewel of wonder, as yet unaware
It had been yielded only on condition
Of whole possession; that it still denied you
Strength or desire for its restitution.

What do you fear? My hand around your throat?
What do I fear? Your dagger through my heart?
Must we not rage alone together
In lofts of singular high starriness?

THE SNAPPED THREAD

Desire, first, by a natural miracle
United bodies, united hearts, blazed beauty;
Transcended bodies, transcended hearts.

Two souls, now unalterably one
In whole love always and for ever,
Soar out of twilight, through upper air,
Let fall their sensuous burden.

Is it kind, though, is it honest even,
To consort with none but spirits—
Leaving true-wedded hearts like ours
In enforced night-long separation,
Each to its random bodily inclination,
The thread of miracle snapped?

FORTUNATE CHILD

For fear strangers might intrude upon us
You and I played at being strangers,
But lent our act such verisimilitude
That when at last, by hazard, we met alone
In a secret glen where the badger earths
We had drawn away from love: did not prepare
For melting of eyes into hearts of flowers,
For a sun-aureoled enhancement of hair,
For over-riding of death on an eagle's back—

Yet so it was: sky shuddered apart before us
Until, from a cleft of more than light, we both
Overheard the laugh of a fortunate child
Swung from those eagle talons in a gold cloth.

LOVING TRUE, FLYING BLIND

How often have I said before
That no soft 'if', no 'either-or',
Can keep my obdurate male mind
From loving true and flying blind?—

Which, though deranged beyond all cure
Of temporal reason, knows for sure
That timeless magic first began
When woman bared her soul to man.

Be bird, be blossom, comet, star,
Be paradisal gates ajar,
But still, as woman, bear you must
With who alone endures your trust.

THE NEAR-ECLIPSE

Out shines again the glorious round Sun—
After his near-eclipse when pools of light
Thrown on the turf between leaf-shadows
Grew crescent-shaped like moons—dizzying us
With paraboles of colour: regal amends
To our own sun mauled barbarously
By the same wide-mouthed dragon.

DANCING FLAME

Pass now in metaphor beyond birds,
Their seasonal nesting and migration,
Their airy gambols, their repetitive song;
Beyond the puma and the ocelot
That spring in air and follow us with their eyes;
Beyond all creatures but our own selves,
Eternal genii of dancing flame
Armed with the irreproachable secret
Of love, which is: never to turn back.

BIRTH OF ANGELS

Never was so profound a shadow thrown
On earth as by your sun: a black roundel
Harbouring an unheard-of generation
Fledged by the sun ablaze above your own—
Wild beyond words, yet each of them an angel.

ON GIVING

Those who dare give nothing
Are left with less than nothing;
Dear heart, you give me everything,
Which leaves you more than everything—
Though those who dare give nothing
Might judge it left you nothing.

Giving you everything,
I too, who once had nothing,
Am left with more than everything
As gifts for those with nothing
Who need, if not our everything,
At least a loving something.

Part 9

THE PERFECTIONISTS

Interalienation of their hearts
It was not, though both played resentful parts
In stern unwillingness to share
One house, one pillow, the same fare.
It was perfectionism, they confess,
To learn the truth and ask for nothing less.

Their fire-eyed guardians watched from overhead:
'These two alone have learned to love', they said,
'But still cannot forget
Neither is worthy of the other yet'.

LION-GENTLE

Love, never disavow our vow
Nor wound your lion-gentle:
Take what you will, dote on it, keep it,
But pay your debts with a grave, wilful smile
Like a woman of the sword.

THE WORD

The Word is unspoken
Between honest lovers:
They substitute a silence
Or wave at a wild flower,
Sighing inaudibly.

That it exists indeed
Will scarcely be disputed:
The wildest of conceptions
Can be reduced to speech—
Or so the Schoolmen teach.

You and I, thronged by angels,
Learned it in the same dream
Which startled us by moonlight,
And that we still revere it
Keeps our souls aflame.

'God' is a standing question
That still negates an answer;
The Word is not a question
But simple affirmation,
The antonym of 'God'.

Who would believe this Word
Could have so long been hidden
Behind a candid smile,
A sweet but hasty kiss,
And always dancing feet?

THE NECKLACE

Variegated flowers, nuts, cockle-shells
And pebbles, chosen lovingly and strung
On golden spider's webs with a gold clasp
For your neck, naturally; and each bead touched
By a boy's lips as he stoops over them:
Wear these for the new miracle they announce—
All four cross-quarter-days beseech you—
Your safe return from shipwreck, drought and war,
Beautiful as before, to what you are.

A BRACELET

A bracelet invisible
For your busy wrist,
Twisted from silver
Spilt afar,
From silver of the clear Moon,
From her sheer halo,
From the male beauty
Of a shooting star.

WHILE THE SKY BLACKENS

Lightning enclosed by a vast ring of mirrors,
Instant thunder extravagantly bandied
Between red cliffs no hawk may nest upon,
Triumphant jetting, passion of deluge: ours—
With spray that stuns, dams that lurch and are gone;
Yet against this insensate hubbub of subsidence
Our voices, ever true to a fireside tone,
Meditate on the secret marriage of flowers
Or the bees' paradise, with much else more,
And while the sky blackens anew for rain
On why we love as none ever loved before.

SUN-FACE AND MOON-FACE

We twin cherubs above the Mercy Seat,
Sun-face and Moon-face,
Locked in the irrevocable embrace
That guards our children from defeat,
Are fire not flesh; as none will dare deny
Lest his own soul should die.

PRISON WALLS

Love, this is not the way
To treat a glorious day:
To cloud it over with conjectured fears,
Wiping my eyes before they brim with tears
And, long before we part,
Mourning the torments of my jealous heart.

That you have tried me more
Than who else did before
Is no good reason to prognosticate
A last ordeal, when I must greet with hate
Your phantom fairy prince
Conjured in childhood, lost so often since.

Nor can a true heart rest
Resigned to second best—
Why did you need to temper me so true
That I became your sword or swords, if you
Must nail me on your wall
And choose a painted lath when the blows fall?

Because I stay heart-whole,
Because you bound your soul
To mine, with curses should it wander free,
I charge you now to keep full faith with me
Nor can I ask for less
Than your unswerving single-heartedness.

Then grieve no more, but while
Your flowers are scented, smile
And never sacrifice, as others may,
So clear a dawn to dread of Judgement Day—
Lest prison walls should see
Fresh tears of longing that you shed for me.

A DREAM OF HELL

You reject the rainbow
Of our Sun Castle
As hyperbolic;

You enjoin the Moon
Of our pure trysts
To condone deceit;

Lured to violence
By a lying spirit,
You break our troth.

Seven wide, enchanted
Wards of horror
Lie stretched before you,

To brand your naked breast
With impious colours,
To band your thighs.

How can I discharge
Your confused spirit
From its chosen hell?

You who once dragged me
From the bubbling slime
Of a tidal reach,

Who washed me, fed me,
Laid me in white sheets,
Warmed me in brown arms,

Would you have me cede
Our single sovereignty
To your tall demon?

OUR SELF

Every reasonable argument
Separates us—are we unreasonable?
We agree to absence but, although communing
Across wide waters, miss each other's voices
And bodies, being resident in bodies.
Our letters read, at best, only as sighs.

The case grows worse and simpler with disorder:
However reasonably we oppose
That unquiet integer, our self, we lose.

HOODED FLAME

Child, though I sorrow, I shall never grieve.
Grief is to mourn a flame extinguished;
Sorrow, to find it hooded for the hour
When planetary influences deceive
And hope, like wine, turns sour.

CROWN OF STARS

Lion-heart, you prowl alone
True to Virgin, Bride and Crone;
None so black of brow as they
Now, tomorrow, yesterday.
Yet the night you shall not see
Must illuminate all three
When the tears of love you shed
Blaze about their single head
And a sword shall pierce the side
Of true Virgin, Crone and Bride
Among mansions of the dead.

PRIDE OF LOVE

I face impossible feats at your desire,
Resentful at the tears of love you shed
For the faint-hearted sick who flock to you;
But since all love lies wholly in the giving
Weep on: your tears are true.
Nor can despair provoke me to self-pity
Where pride alone is due.

Song: THE PALM TREE

Palm-tree, single and apart
    In your serpent-haunted land,
Like the fountain of a heart
    Soaring into air from sand—
None can count it as a fault
That your roots are fed with salt.

Panniers-full of dates you yield,
    Thorny branches laced with light,
Wistful for no pasture field
    Fed by torrents from a height,
Short of politics to share
With the damson or the pear.

Never-failing Phoenix-tree
    In your serpent-haunted land,
Fount of magic soaring free
    From this desert of salt sand;
Tears of joy are salty too—
Mine shall flow in praise of you.

IF AND WHEN

She hates an *if*, know that for sure:
Whether in cunning or self-torture,
Your *ifs* anticipate the *when*
That womankind conceals from men.

IN PERSPECTIVE

What, keep love *in perspective?*—that old lie
Forced on the Imagination by the Eye
Which, mechanistically controlled, will tell
How rarely table-sides run parallel;
How distance shortens us; how wheels are found
Oval in shape far oftener than round;
How every ceiling-corner's out of joint;
How the broad highway tapers to a point—
Can all this fool us lovers? Not for long:
Even the blind will sense that something's wrong.

INJURIES

Injure yourself, you injure me:
Is that not true as true can be?
Nor can you give me cause to doubt
It works the other way about—
Then what precautions need I take
Not to be injured for Love's sake?

THE BOWER BIRD

The Bower-bird improvised a cool retreat
For the hen's pleasure, doing his poor best
With parrot's plumage, orchids, bones and corals,
To enchant her fancy—but this was no nest . . .
So though the Penguin laid at his hen's feet
An egg-shaped pebble, pleading: 'Be my bride',
And though the Jackdaw's nest was glorified
With stolen rings and brooches massed inside,
It was the Bower-bird who contented me
By not equating love with matrimony.

MIST

Fire and Deluge, rival pretenders
To ruling the world's end; these cannot daunt us
Whom flames will never singe, nor floods drown,
While we stand guard against their murderous child
Mist, that slyly catches at love's throat,
Shrouding the clear sun and clean waters
Of all green gardens everywhere—
The twitching mouths likewise and furtive eyes
Of those who speak us fair.

BITES AND KISSES

Heather and holly,
Bites and kisses,
A courtship-royal
On the hill's red cusp.
Look up, look down,
Gaze all about you—
A livelier world
By ourselves contrived:

Swan in full course
Up the Milky Way,
Moon in her wildness,
Sun ascendant
In Crab or Lion,
Beyond the bay
A pride of dolphins
Curving and tumbling
With bites and kisses . . .

Or dog-rose petals
Well-starred by dew
Or jewelled pebbles,
Or waterlilies open
For the dragon-flies
In their silver and blue.

SPITE OF MIRRORS

O what astonishment if you
Could see yourself as others do,
Foiling the mirror's wilful spite
That shows your left cheek as the right
And shifts your lovely crooked smile
To the wrong corner! But meanwhile
Lakes, pools and puddles all agree
(Bound in a vast conspiracy)
To yield no more than your set look
Designed for peering in a book—
No easy laugh, no glint of rage,
No thoughts in passionate pilgrimage,
Nor start of guilt, nor rising fear,
Nor premonition of a tear.

And how, with mirrors, can you keep
Watch on your eyelids closed in sleep?
How judge which profile to bestow
On a new coin or cameo?
How from two steps behind you, stare
At your firm nape discovered bare
Of ringlets, as you bend and reach
Transparent pebbles from the beach?
So if you long for the surprise
Of self-discernment, hold my eyes
And plunge far down in them to see
Sights never long withheld from me.

HER BRIEF WITHDRAWAL

'Forgive me, love, if I withdraw awhile:
It is only that you ask such bitter questions,
Always another beyond the extreme last.
And the answers astound. You have entangled me
In my own mystery. Grant me a respite.
I was happier far, not asking, nor much caring,
Choosing by appetite only: self-deposed,
Self-reinstated, no one observing.
While I belittled this vibrancy of touch
And the active vengeance of these folded arms
No one could certify my powers for me
Or my saining virtue, or know that I compressed
Knots of destiny in a careless fist:
I who passed for a foundling from the hills,
Of innocent and flower-like phantasies,
Though minting silver by my mere tread . . .
Did I not dote on you, I well might strike you
For implicating me in your true dream'.

THE CRANE

The Crane lounes loudly in his need,
    And so for love I loune:
Son to the sovereign Sun indeed,
    Courier to the Moon.

STRANGENESS

You love me strangely, and in strangeness
I love you wholly, with no parallel
To this long miracle, for each example
Of love coincidence levels a finger
At strangeness undesigned as unforeseen.

And this long miracle is to discover
The inmost you and never leave her;
To nurse no curiosity for another;
To forge the soul and its desire together
Gently, openly and forever.

Seated in silence, clothed in silence
And face to face—the room is small
But thronged with visitants—
We ask for nothing: we have all.

SHE TO HIM

To have it, sweetheart, is to know you have it
Rather than think you have it;
To think you have it is a wish to take it—
Though afterwards you will not have it—
And thus a fear to take it.
Yet if you know you have it, you may take it
And know that still you have it.

Song: CHERRIES OR LILIES

Death can have no alternative but Love,
Or Love but Death.
Acquaintance dallying on the path of Love,
Sickness on that of Death,
Pause at a bed-side, doing what they can
With fruit and flowers bought from the barrow man.

Death can have no alternative but Love,
Or Love but Death.
Then shower me cherries from your orchard, Love,
Or pluck me lilies, Death:
For she and I were never of that breed
Who vacillate or trifle with true need.

FOR EVER

Sweetheart, I beg you to renew and seal
With a not supererogatory kiss
Our contract of 'For Ever.'
                              Learned judges
Deplore the household sense 'interminable':
True love, they rule, never acknowledges
Future or past, only a perfect now . . .
But let it read 'For Ever', anyhow!

Song: DEW-DROP AND DIAMOND

The difference between you and her
(Whom I to you did once prefer)
Is clear enough to settle:
She like a diamond shone, but you
Shine like an early drop of dew
Poised on a red rose petal.

The dew-drop carries in its eye
Mountain and forest, sea and sky,
With every change of weather;
Contrariwise, a diamond splits
The prospect into idle bits
That none can piece together.

TO BE IN LOVE

To spring impetuously in air and remain
Treading on air for three heart-beats or four,
Thence to descend at leisure; or else to climb
A forward-tilted crag with no hand-holds;
Or, disembodied, to carry jasmine back
From a Queen's garden—this is being in love,
Armed with *agilitas* and *subtilitas*,
At which few famous lovers even guessed,
Though children may foreknow it, deep in dreams,
And ghosts may mourn it, haunting their own tombs,
And peacocks cry it, in default of speech.

THE OLIVE YARD

Now by a sudden shift of eye
The hitherto exemplary world
Takes on immediate wildness,
And birds, trees, winds, the characters
Of our childhood's alphabet, alter
Into rainbowed mysteries.

Flesh is no longer flesh, but power;
Numbers, no longer arithmetical,
Dance like lambs, fly like doves;
And silence falls at last, though silken branches
Gently heave in the near oliveyard
And vague cloud labours on.

Whose was the stroke of summer genius
Dealt from a mountain fastness
Where the griffon vulture soars,
That let us read our always shrouded future
As easily as a book of prayer
Spread open on the knee?

THE YET UNSAYABLE

It was always fiercer, brighter, gentler than could be told
Even in words quickened by Truth's dark eye:
Its absence, whirlpool; its presence, deluge;
Its time, astonishment; its magnitude,
A murderous dagger-point.
                              So we surrender
Our voices to the dried and scurrying leaves
And choose our own long-predetermined path
From the unsaid to the yet unsayable
In silence of love and love's temerity.

THE NARROW SEA

With you for mast and sail and flag,
And anchor never known to drag,
Death's narrow but oppressive sea
Looks not unnavigable to me.

WITHIN REASON

You have wandered widely through your own mind
And your own perfect body;
Thus learning, within reason, gentle one,
Everything that can prove worth the knowing.

A concise wisdom never attained by those
Bodiless nobodies
Who travel pen in hand through others' minds,
But without reason,
Feeding on manifold contradiction.

To stand perplexed by love's inconsequences,
Like fire-flies in your hair
Or distant flashes of a summer storm:
Such are the stabs of joy you deal me
Who also wander widely through my mind
And still imperfect body.

Index